Treasures

In Grief

D1519385

Discover 7 Spiritual Gifts

Hidden in Your Pain

Love 'n Light,
Lo Anne Mayer

Lo Anne Mayer

Defining Moments Press, Inc.

Copyright © Lo Anne Mayer, 2023

Brand and product names are trademarks or registered trademarks of their respective owners.

Defining Moments ™ is a registered Trademark

Cover Design: 99 Designs

Editing: Amber Torres

Table of Contents

Lo Anne Mayer

Dedication for Treasures in Grief

To my mother, Lois Janes, who opened the door
to Transpersonal Journaling for me.

To my daughter, Cyndi Idleman, who taught me
that Love Never Dies.

To my daughter, Karen Loenser, without whom
this book would never have been published.

Foreword
Treasures in Grief

By: Gloria Horsley, President and Founder of Open to Hope

Loss and grief are universal experiences that all of us encounter in our lives. While the journey of coping with and overcoming grief is unique to each individual, hearing about others' experiences and struggles can be a vital part of the healing process. Books such as Victor Frankl's Man's Search for Meaning, in which he shares his own story of losing his family in the Holocaust, have inspired millions of people. Similarly, Lo Anne Mayer courageously tells her personal story in Treasures in Grief, including her spiritual connections with deceased loved ones. Sharing personal stories of grief is an important aspect of helping others cope with their losses. As someone who has experienced profound loss, I have found solace and healing in hearing thousands of stories through my foundation, Open to Hope. Lo Anne's journey through the loss of her daughter Cyndi inspires me with the goodness of humanity and the willingness to discuss the spiritual aspects of the grieving process and the connections we can have with those who have passed away. I believe that Treasures in Grief and the Seven Spiritual Gifts Hidden in Your Pain will help many individuals navigate their own grief experiences.

Lo Anne's book, Treasures in Grief, is especially poignant as she shares the loss of her daughter Cyndi to suicide and the additional burden of being deprived of seeing her grandchildren due to her son-in-law's anger. This book is a continuation of her first book, Celestial Conversations, in which she explores how transpersonal journaling helped her connect with her deceased mother and daughter. Through workshops and her previous book, Lo Anne has already made a significant impact on the lives of thousands of people. In Treasures in Grief, she takes readers on her personal journey, sharing childhood experiences and the events that shaped her path. The book outlines her healing process, which was facilitated by the spiritual gifts she miraculously received: courage, compassion, faith, spiritual expansion, forgiveness, unconditional love, and mission. It unveils the unexpected treasures that can be found within the dark night of the soul that follows a loss.

Lo Anne is not a traditional Catholic, and she approaches the spiritual realms in her own unique way. Even if readers may initially be skeptical, they will enjoy hearing her perspective on the world and her approach, characterized by integrity, honesty, and courage. She embodies someone who marches to the beat of their own drum while remaining compassionate and caring, simultaneously healing herself and others along the way. One of the most admirable aspects of Lo Anne's journey is her constant quest for post-traumatic growth. Like my daughter, Heidi, who transformed the loss of her brother into a mission advocating for sibling grief, Lo Anne exemplifies finding purpose and mission in the midst of tragedy and chaos. It is worth noting that there may be an eighth spiritual gift that Lo Anne imparts through this book: the gift of healing.

Treasures in Grief: Discover 7 Spiritual Gifts Hidden in Your Pain by Lo Anne Mayer is a deeply insightful and inspiring book that guides readers through the journey of grief, revealing the spiritual gifts that can be found within the process of healing. Mayer's personal experiences and her unique approach to spirituality make this book a valuable resource for anyone grappling with loss. Her courage, compassion, and unwavering search for growth and purpose offer solace and hope to those who are navigating their own paths of grief. Ultimately, Mayer's book is a testament to the power of resilience and the transformative potential of embracing our pain to find hidden treasures within.

Introduction

When our daughter, Cyndi, died, I began a long journey of grief that involved transpersonal journaling with her as well as with my Mother, who had died the year before. My transpersonal journaling with Cyndi and Mom allowed me to reach through the veil of death to ask questions. The information I received was essential to my own healing and produced my first book, Celestial Conversations: Healing Relationships After Death.

Twelve years later, my book had developed into workshops all over the US and I was on my way to England to give a retreat with two of my co-founders of the International Grief Council. As I prepared for the trip, I remembered that Glastonbury, England was not far from where we were giving the retreat. It was then that I decided to go back to Glastonbury for closure, since that was where I was when I received the phone call that our daughter, Cyndi, had died.

In the process of returning to the place where I suffered my PTSD, I discovered something important. I took the time to look back over the thirteen years of trying to recover from the death of my child only to discover that my soul had grown immensely! To my amazement, I found that I had received seven spiritual gifts as I moved through my grief.

I never noticed these treasures as I struggled to recover and find purpose from the death of our daughter. I encourage you, dear reader, to walk with me during my discovery. You may find that you, too, have received "extraordinary gifts" from Grief.

Love and Light,
Lo Anne

Chapter 1
Returning to Glastonbury

"Grief can be the garden of compassion. If you keep your heart open through everything, your pain can become your greatest ally in your lifetimes search for love and wisdom."
- Rumi

Excitement coursed through my veins as I anticipated my appointment in Glastonbury, England. Thirteen years had passed since I stood in this exact spot. I couldn't resist sprinting up High Street and turning right on Wells Road. I slowed down from fear and perspiration on this hot August morning as I approached my destination. The shock of seeing the Abbey House through its huge gate was overwhelming. I leaned against the ten-foot-high stone wall that surrounded the property. I needed to catch my breath and focus on why I came. The charcoal-gray stones were cool and refreshing on my back after my fifteen-minute dash from my B&B. My legs refused to move any further. An invisible guard kept me stock-still as I absorbed the sight of my own post-traumatic stress experience.

My mind flooded with the memories of leaving the Abbey House in a daze on July 20, 2005. I could see myself being gently placed in a taxi, while a crowd of tearful women surrounded me on the front steps of this same building.

On that same day, most of the women in my writers' retreat had gone to visit a crop circle nearby. I chose to stay home and participate in the labyrinth meditation. During the meditation, I felt a strong urge to call my family in NJ. I hurried upstairs to the second floor of the Abbey to make the call. The lobster-red telephone sat on a table in the hallway. Since I had no cell phone, I poured out the change I needed to make the call. I couldn't wait to thank my husband for encouraging me to make the trip: I had fallen in love with Glastonbury.

The Moment My Life Changed Forever

The minute our daughter, Diane, picked up the phone, I launched into an enthusiastic narrative of the land of Camelot. She interrupted me with words that would change me forever. "Mom, Cyndi is dead. You must come home."

I couldn't move, let alone comprehend what Diane had said. Just then, all the change I had fed into the phone was swallowed up, and it went silent. I turned to the woman next to me and blurted out, "Diane said my daughter is dead. That can't be right."

Susan emptied all her change on the telephone table and gently said, "Call her back." My hands shook violently as I dialed the number. My husband answered. Through his tears he confirmed that our daughter, Cyndi, was found dead in her bed at home in NJ that very morning. I remained frozen in my chair. The handset of the phone was still in my hand as I struggled to comprehend what I had heard. Susan flew down the stairs to find help.

I needed to do something, but what? I mumbled, "I must go home," as I hurried down the hall to my room. I threw items haphazardly into my suitcase and collapsed onto the bed in tears.

The Abbey House manager knocked politely but firmly on the door and walked in. With deep sorrow in his eyes, John said, "I have a taxi waiting; I changed your airline ticket to tomorrow morning, made reservations at the Radisson Hotel at Heathrow Airport for tonight and Karen, will meet you there." Karen, our oldest daughter, had been sent to London on her first and only assignment by her employer during the same week I had chosen to participate in my writers' retreat in Glastonbury. How grateful I was to know that she would fly home with me.

I said nothing, only comprehending that this kind and caring man was helping me to go home; he waited for me to walk out the door ahead of him, as he picked up my suitcase. I grabbed my purse and gripped the banister tightly as I descended the stairs to the front door. I could see the tears in the eyes of the women who were my fellow retreatants, but no one said a word; neither did I. The silence was deafening.

Coming Back to Glastonbury

My mind suddenly brought me back to the present.

"Could that have been thirteen years ago?" I mumbled out loud to my friend, Juliane. The memory of the phantom taxi driving through the Abbey Gate towards the highway to Heathrow Airport slowly faded, and I returned to the current time.

Juliane didn't respond. She had come with me to explore the Abbey House. She is a psychotherapist with her own practice in Germany. We became email friends years earlier, after the publication of my book, Celestial Conversations: Healing Relations After Death in 2011.

She had been introduced to me by Graham Maxey, who had written the foreword of my book. Juliane Grodhues had been trained, along with Graham, by Dr. Allan Botkin to work with veterans who suffered from PTSD using Induced After Death Communication (IADC).

On this day, Juliane and I became life-long friends. Her training and compassion were perfect for me as I returned to find closure in Glastonbury. She slipped her arm through mine and gently nudged me toward the front door of the Abbey House. "It's eleven o'clock. They are probably waiting for you," she said. Juliane's encouragement brought me back to reality and the purpose of my visit.

I deliberately chose to return to Glastonbury in the summer of 2017. As a co-founder of The International Grief Council, I was scheduled to offer a Grief Retreat at a nearby Quaker retreat house in a few days. Uma Girish (born in India) and Daniela Norris (born in Israel) and I formed the International Grief Council in 2014 after getting to know one another. We had each lost loved-ones and written books about our grief.

As we became friends, we discovered that, despite having nothing in common other than our grief, we spoke the same language of grief. We began giving talks in the United States and found that the honest expression of our individual grief processes resonated with many people. Our success led to the opportunity to give a Grief Retreat at Charney Manor in Oxford, England. I hoped that returning to Glastonbury prior to the retreat would give me the insight and closure I needed so many years later after Cyndi's death.

As Juliane and I walked seventy-five feet toward the enormous black front door of the Abbey House, I glanced to the left, looking for the labyrinth that had catapulted me into calling home that infamous day in 2005. It was gone! I looked up at the second-floor window on the right of the building that framed my bedroom during my stay years earlier. I recalled how beautiful the garden below looked to me the first time I peered outside. The yellow lilies and red roses that I admired were also gone. All I could see was my own ashen, tear-stained face looking up to the heavens in supplication. Now there were six British cars parked on the pavement that replaced the garden.

Juliane encouraged me to ring the doorbell. No one answered. I rang again. It wasn't possible, after so many emails, that Liam would forget that today was the date and time of my scheduled visit. A heavy-set woman, with her hair pulled severely back in a bun, opened the door. Not a smile or a welcome. She told us to wait in the hall until she found Liam. "I will get Liam ," she announced in a voice as cold as the stones in the wall at the entrance of the driveway.

Retracing My Footsteps From the Past

Juliane and I walked to the center of the immense foyer with its mahogany paneling. Immediately I was drawn into the ornate living room beyond, with its huge windows overlooking the Abbey

25

Monastery. I visualized the twenty women in our writer's retreat sitting in a circle in 2005, as we listened to our leader, Emily Hanlon. The vision was so real that I almost sat down on the floor to join them. Instead, I rested on the window seat to observe my "ghosts from the past." The Abbey House, now the office of the Glastonbury Abbey Trust, no longer allows week-long writers' retreats to be held on its premises. However, I received special permission to come back into the building and walk the grounds for my personal remembrance. I was not permitted to go upstairs to my old room or any place on the second floor because that area now serves as business offices.

Juliane shadowed me as we moved slowly from room to room. I retreated into my memories. "This is where we spent most of our time writing and sharing stories," I pointed out. "We even created wands from sticks and flowers we found on the property. "I still have mine," I said, surprised that the remark sounded so proud to my ears. The yin and yang of my joy and sorrow was coursing through my memory bank.

Liam suddenly appeared. His warm interest in my visit was comforting. He showed us the dining room where we had our meals. It seemed packed with ghosts of the past. I could see the faces of the ladies happily discussing the writings that they were working on. I struggled to remember their names. Liam looked at his watch and suggested that we take a walk outside around the large grounds.

As he ushered us out of the front door, the sunshine seemed especially warm after the cold atmosphere inside the building. I moved directly to the area that housed the huge labyrinth I walked before calling home in 2005. There was no trace of it. As we moved around the back of the Abbey House, my favorite aspen tree called to me. It had grown at least ten feet higher than I remembered. I had sat under that tree to write my assignments and its branches had protected me from the hot summer sun. I sat under it again feeling its branches wrap its arms around me.

Over the wall that surrounded the Abbey House property, we could see the ruins of the Glastonbury Abbey. This Benedictine Abbey has legendary status for being the earliest Christian monastic site in Great Britain. It was established in 900 AD and became the wealthiest Abbey in England. It is reported to be the burial site of King Arthur. The monastery was burned to the ground in 1140 AD, but its majesty and history is part of the mystique of Glastonbury. The factual history of Glastonbury sits alongside the myths of Avalon. I intended to spend hours on the immense grounds of the monastery. There was so much to see and remember from 2005.

As Juliane and I circled our way around the Abbey House property, we sat on the porch garden bench, taking pictures of the pink roses and orange lilies. The Abbey House was built in the nineteenth century by John Fry Reeves, a banker with antiquarian interest and exquisite taste. We could almost see the parties that must have been hosted on this beautiful portico. If only this house could talk. I wasn't inclined to say much during our tour, and Juliane didn't force the issue. She just walked beside me.

When we finished exploring, Juliane and I felt drawn to continue down Wells Road to the Chalice Well. The legend is that the Chalice of Christ was brought there by Joseph of Arimathea after Christ's crucifixion. Joseph supposedly hid the chalice in one of the fifteen wells for safekeeping during the persecution of the Christians in the Holy land. During my writers' retreat in 2005, I made repeated trips to the Chalice Well, where I was told that fairies guard the Chalice. We were encouraged to drink the healing waters at the Chalice Well because many healings have been reported. The Chalice Well was the last place I visited before I flew home to bury Cyndi.

Juliane and I lingered in the shade of the many trees and flowering bushes that make up this magical property. As we dangled our bare feet in the well water on this hot August day, she helped me to articulate what I had just witnessed and what I hoped to accomplish on this trip. My goal was closure after having rushed home from Glastonbury because of Cyndi's death. I also wanted to finish seeing the sights that I missed because I left so quickly. I felt a deep bond with this place. I didn't realize at the time that Glastonbury is also the heart chakra of the world. Once I learned that fact, I realized how appropriate it was that Glastonbury was the site of my broken heart.

I began my own healing through transpersonal journaling with Cyndi and my mother. I discovered that receiving information from my loved-ones on the other side of the veil made a deeper healing possible in my heart. Glastonbury held the key not only to closure, but to a new chapter of my life.

The heat of the day, together with my emotional experience of being back at the Abbey House caught up with me. I decided to leave Juliane and return to the Daisy Centre B&B for rest; I had intended to explore all of the points of interest in Glastonbury, but now I needed to sleep. My knees were buckling.

Juliane ascended the Tor, a timeless hill whose summit provided breathtaking vistas of the idyllic English countryside. Perched atop the Tor, St. Michael's Church, constructed in the fourteenth century, rose majestically. In the distance I could see cows grazing in the meadow.

The trip to the top of the Tor would take at least thirty minutes. The thought of such a strenuous climb felt exhausting; it was too much of an effort for me on this particular day.

Resting at the B&B, I could hear the church bells as I fell asleep.

Past Life Memories with the Queen of Camelot

I woke up to Church bells a few hours later. I felt an urgent need to go to Glastonbury Abbey. As I rushed down Wells Road, past the many little shops filled with crystals and candles, I could smell the incense as I made my way towards it. I hurried on as if I were late for Mass. As I turned left onto Magdalene Street, I could see the entrance to Glastonbury Abbey and lots of people leaving the grounds. A sign indicated that the premises would close at 5:00 pm and it was already 4:00 pm; there was no way I could see everything in one hour. Nevertheless, I paid the nine pounds and went inside.

I walked straight towards a crowd gathered around one of the docents who was dressed in the attire of the twelfth century. I found myself standing at the grave of King Arthur himself. The docent was discussing how Arthur and another small-boned woman with golden hair were found by those who were excavating the Abbey.

Suddenly, I remembered a story that I wrote in 2005 about a nun who worked in the kitchen of Glastonbury Abbey. As I stood there, I relived the image of that same nun. In my reverie, I followed the vision as she appeared to walk across the field to the kitchen which was being renovated at the time.

Now I clearly remembered the story I had written under the aspen tree on the Abbey House property in 2005. I realized that it was a past-life memory that I recounted. This was the same ghostly nun that had been so kind to me when I came to the Abbey many lifetimes ago. She had been my teacher and trained me to become an acceptable cook. Most of all, she had confided to me how difficult it was for her to adapt to life as a nun after being the Queen of Camelot!

As I recalled the story, I deliberately moved away from the crowd. I found a quiet spot on the Abbey grounds in order to further recall the story that I had written in 2005. Moving deeper into my past life experience, I envisioned who I now recognized as Sr. Mary Martha opening the gate to the Abbey. Eyes cast down, she whispered, "Praise be Jesus Christ." In my dream state, I heard myself saying, "Sister, I have come to meet you and recall my past life experience here in Glastonbury. The Mother

Prioress has given me permission to speak with you."

Torn between the Mother Prioress' directive and what seemed to be her own fear, Sr. Mary Martha said nothing, and opened the gate to let me in. Then she turned away from me, leading me in silence into the chapel. I followed. The chapel was quiet and dark. Sr. Mary Martha walked directly down the main aisle, genuflected and slipped into a pew in front of the statue of The Blessed Mother. I followed, stopping a few pews behind her on the right side. My seat creaked loudly as I sat down. I am aware that Sr. Mary Martha made no sound at all as she slipped down the aisle ahead of me and knelt to pray. I reflected that her knees made no dent in the felt kneeler. She was such a rail of a woman.

As my past life memory unfolded, the nun made no sound but her lips moved quickly in prayer. Her mouth was pursed in between Aves, as she proceeded to pray with her eyes closed for ten minutes by my watch. In reverence for her fear and surprise, I waited, not thinking to pray myself. I watched her unmoving, rigid body. I couldn't see her eyes, but something told me that tears rolled down her scrawny cheeks. She didn't pull out a handkerchief or acknowledge those tears in any way. I could feel her frustration. Tears are a sign of weakness! Inappropriate for a nun or a queen. So many unshed tears. Poor Guinevere! "Is she afraid to shed one tear, lest they turn into torrents?" I wondered.

Finally, Sr. Mary Martha stood up, moved to the center of the aisle, genuflected on both knees. She then looked me straight in the eyes, nodded and turned to leave the chapel. Once again, I followed. Down the aisle, out the heavy oak door, which she held open for me without a word. She walked across the sunlit courtyard to another door. Turning to see if I understood to follow her, she led me inside. I walked into a library with dark mahogany panels and bookshelves that were filled from floor to ceiling with books. It felt just like the chapel I had left. In the quiet I could hear the nuns chanting in the distance. My eyes were drawn to the picture of the Madonna and Child above her. Such a stone-faced mother. I wondered if the Queen would have been as cold a mother if she had borne a child.

"You have come to interview me." Sister Mary Martha's voice was regal with a touch of anger. "I can only give you a little time as we go into Evensong in a short time."

"I am so sorry that Mother Prioress Eunice did not warn you of my arrival, Sister. It must be a shock to have me here."

"Mother Prioress has not been well for a week. I have not seen her. Perhaps she meant to tell me."

37

Sister Mary Martha's voice drifted off. I knew that Mother Prioress rarely spoke to her.

Producing a letter with Mother Prioress Eunice's imprimatur, I handed it to Sr. Mary Martha. She read it and nodded, handing it back to me. "I didn't want you to feel I was an imposter, Sister," I said. "This is a very important opportunity for me. I recognize the gift of your time as a great honor. Besides, I want you to feel comfortable with me… and not at all afraid."

"Time is all I have, my dear. Time with the Lord. Silence, prayer, memories, regrets and reparation. How can I help you, my daughter?"

"I would like to write a story about your experience here. I think the world would benefit from your story of your life as Queen Guinevere. Would you allow me to share it?"

"Camelot lives on without our help," said Sister Mary Martha quietly. "The truth is relative. I don't think the truth will change anything. However, because you have asked, I will pray over it. I will contact you if I change my mind. In the meantime, seek YOUR truth here at the Abbey. What is YOUR truth? How can it help you in this life? I feel that is the real reason why you are here."

With that, the vision vanished. My reverie ended as quickly as it arrived. I sat down on a large boulder to try to collect myself in the present time. The loudspeaker announced it was closing time. I was one of the last to leave the Abbey grounds.

Little did I know all that I would eventually remember, learn and come to understand. This was the beginning of my journey into the seven spiritual gifts of grief.

Chapter 2
The Spiritual Gifts Revealed

"A good friend is like a four-leaf clover: hard to find and lucky to have"
- An Irish Proverb

Back at the B&B, I found Juliane, who suggested that we go to dinner at the Hundred Monkeys Café. I shared my vision at the Abbey and we talked for hours about my hopes and plans for this visit to Glastonbury. That dinner solidified our friendship. I was so grateful for Juliane's wisdom and professional experience with individuals who had suffered from Post Traumatic Stress Disorder as I had. She understood me and my journey. I couldn't have asked for a more perfect companion as we discussed the places and experiences we could explore. Juliane encouraged me to move slowly through my next four days and to be open to insights that could help me.

The next morning, as we were walking to the Glastonbury Thorn Tree, which sits on Wearyall Hill overlooking Glastonbury, Juliane asked me what I had learned from my grief. It was a deep question that couldn't be answered quickly or succinctly. Because the hill was very steep, I found talking was exhausting while we climbed. Nevertheless, I pondered her question.

Again, it was the historical significance of my surroundings that inspired me. I thought about the hundreds of years that had passed since Joseph of Arimathea arrived in Glastonbury. The legend was that he was fleeing Jerusalem with other Christians after the death of Christ. Joseph had chosen to return to Glastonbury where he had lived years before, and in those earlier days, Joseph had brought a young Jesus Christ with him.

I pondered the grief that Joseph and his friends must have been feeling as they fled Jerusalem after the death of their Messiah. And, how legend also says that they brought the Holy Grail with them. They called this place Wearyall Hill because they were totally exhausted from their journey. When Joseph arrived, he planted his walking stick into the ground and fell asleep. When he woke up the stick had flowered and has flowered every Christmas and Spring since.

I felt that same exhaustion when Cyndi died. Her death had gutted me like a fish. I also recognized that my own life had flowered like the Glastonbury Thorn Tree after I wrote my book, Celestial Conversations: Healing Relationships After Death.

Like the tree, the blossoms in my life came from overcoming the grief that came from unexpected places. I had been emotionally abused by some individuals who didn't believe in my conversations with my Mother and Cyndi. Quite a few of the people with whom I shared my story rolled their eyes when they heard about reaching through the veil. Others verbally confessed that my premise for transpersonal journaling was impossible. I felt deeply disappointed and tempted not to publish the book. However, my publisher, Lorraine Ash, promised me that readers would not only relate to my story, but would find hope and healing from the information I was sharing. She went on to state that if I wrote the book, it would heal me. The book was published in 2011 and that's when the blossoming in my own life began.

Soon I was invited to give workshops on how to use transpersonal journaling. In each of my workshops, I thanked my publisher, Lorraine Ash, for encouraging me. Watching the faces of the participants when they received information from their dead loved-ones brought tears to my eyes. I felt so blessed that I had persisted with my book and those precious workshops. A Gift of Grief became obvious to me at that moment. I had courage! More courage than ever before! I pondered my new awareness as Juliane and I continued our climb up the steep hill. Like many other grieving parents, I had spent so many years trying to survive my grief that I never stopped to think about the gifts I had been given BECAUSE of my grief.

While we were together in Glastonbury, Juliane and I talked about how Cyndi's death changed the trajectory of my life. As a cradle Catholic, I would never have believed that an ordinary person, like myself, could reach through the veil and talk to a loved-one who had died. And yet I had done so with my daughter and my mother for over eight years at that point. Being able to receive information about situations that puzzled me directly from my deceased mother and my deceased daughter had been instrumental in helping me heal my own broken heart.

In her professional life as a psychologist, Juliane spent years using a process called "Induced After Death Conversations" with her clients in Germany. This process was developed by Dr. Allan Botkin in 1995, a clinical psychologist in the United States. Because of her training, Juliane was not at all surprised that I could write to my mother and daughter. Nor was she stunned by the information they gave me in return. It was so comforting to be with her.

On our way back to our B&B from Wearyall Hill, we stopped at St. Margaret's chapel on Magdalen Street which was founded in 900 AD. There was a hospital next to the chapel that included ten tiny rooms and an exquisite garden that took my breath away. The tiny chapel invited us in. I continued to pray about Juliane's question, "What have you learned from your grief?"

In one of the rooms there was a display of a photographer's passion for orbs. Some say that orbs are transparent balls of light energy that are connected to spirits. Previously, I had only heard about orbs from a couple of friends. The pictures on display clearly showed orbs that were making themselves known in the fifty pictures taken in Britain. The pictures were beautiful, even magical. There is so much we don't know, and yet the possibilities were all around us! I couldn't help but reflect upon that.

The spiritual atmosphere of St Margaret's chapel grounds seemed palpable. The garden was beautifully tended with lilies and roses with an exquisitely carved wooden bench that invited me to rest for a while. After our long walk to and from Wearyall Hill, this was a delightful respite. I was grateful to be able to take time to reflect on everything I was feeling and learning.

On my way out of the grounds, I stopped again inside the tiny chapel. Over the candle-lit altar a list appeared to me. The words seemed to be written in gold above the altar. I blinked, wondering if I was the only one who could see them. Juliane had gone ahead and I was all alone. I sat down in the nearest chair in the tiny chapel to absorb the meaning of the words, which I knew were just for me to see.

There was no one in the chapel to corroborate what I saw. And yet, the serenity of the place seemed to wrap me with angel wings. I savored these moments as I meditated on each one:

COURAGE

COMPASSION

FAITH

SPIRITUAL EXPANSION

FORGIVENESS

UNCONDITIONAL LOVE

MISSION

These, I knew in that moment, were my seven spiritual gifts of grief.

Mesmerized by this vision, I prayed that the Good Lord would help me accept my gifts at a soul level. I needed to understand the meaning before I could breathe a word to anyone. I kept pondering the list days later as I moved on to the grief retreat at Charney Manor followed by my return to the United States. It has taken me fourteen years to understand the gifts that I received BECAUSE of the heartbreak I endured.

As I contemplated these spiritual gifts, I began to realize that I had received renewed courage after Cyndi died. It took courage to publish my book. And yet it has helped hundreds of people over the years. I felt a deep connection to God in this chapel. I recognized that my faith in God was deeper and wider than at any time in my life. While I couldn't hear the voice of God, I had begun to use my transpersonal journaling with God.

As I sat in St. Margaret's chapel I finally recognized how much my spiritual vision had grown since Cyndi died. Like the connecting pools at the Chalice Well, each word in my vision spilled into the next. They would continue to be my teachers.

Spiritual Gift #1 - COURAGE

Spiritual Gift #2 - COMPASSION

Spiritual Gift #3 - FAITH

Spiritual Gift #4 - SPIRITUAL EXPANSION

Spiritual Gift #5 - FORGIVENESS

Spiritual Gift #6 - UNCONDITIONAL LOVE

Spiritual Gift #7 - MISSION

As Juliane and I headed back to the B&B, my head was in a cloud of knowing. I thought about these seven spiritual gifts with new eyes. What about the other gifts that came directly from my grief? I took some time to rest and reflect before dinner. The result of my meditative rest was my decision to meditate on each gift.

Using my journal I began a process that has taken me years. In the following chapters I will give you the results of my investigation. I hope they will inspire you to consider discovering your own gifts from grief.

Chapter 3
Spiritual Gift #1 - Courage

"Courage is one step ahead of fear"
- Deavita

My Lineage of Courage

I learned courage at my mother's knee. Lois Lang was born in 1917 when the world was at war. She married a cadet at West Point the day Hitler marched into Poland. She lived the life of a military wife for fifteen years, moving twenty times, bearing a daughter and a son, enduring two miscarriages in between live births. She kept the home-fires burning when my father was sent to Burma. She typed the manuscript for The Price of Survival, a book which my father helped Brigadier General

Joseph Sweet write while Dad worked at the Pentagon. Neither my mother nor my father got credit for the book that they both put together for the General. Mom carried her husband's personal pain after he viewed the atrocities of the North Koreans on our military soldiers when he served on the Panmunjong Peace treaties in Korea. Finally, she endured her own solitary devastation when my father filed for divorce.

It took immense courage for a Catholic woman in the fifties to be divorced. The church didn't support her. Her family blamed her for "letting the marriage disintegrate." She never said a word against anyone. She simply slipped into a deep depression. Eventually she realized she had to create a new life for her two children. She moved home with her parents and got a job. Never complaining, she kept her pain tightly wrapped in her heart. She never shared any of her heartache with me. My mother had immense courage.

Finding Courage From Within

My own courage was tested many times while raising six children, but never so much as when Cyndi died. Losing a child is gut-wrenching. I never had an inkling that Cyndi would even consider taking her own life. I certainly couldn't believe that she died by suicide, even though that is listed on her death certificate.

I honestly did not believe that I had enough strength to face life after Cyndi died. A life that entailed re-telling the story of her death to all of the people who asked, "What happened?" The courage that was needed to say, "I can't talk about it right now." The courage to live through the countless sleepless nights and horrendous nightmares of not being with her as she died while I was in England. For many people who are grieving, just going to bed takes courage. The nightmares make you afraid to sleep, even though you need to sleep desperately.

Inch by inch, I developed courage that I honestly didn't know I had. It took courage to go to the wake and the funeral. Cyndi's husband was there. I felt he was the enemy. It was a nightmare just being in the same room with him. It took courage to go to our church where hundreds of people attended Cyndi's funeral Mass. The anguish we experienced at her gravesite during Cyndi's burial required extraordinary courage. And yet, our family was able to pick out a perfect gravesite and have a beautiful service and repast. I could hardly believe we got through it all! Most of our children came from all over the United States. Our son, Raymond Jr had to fly in from Japan for the service. All of us found as much courage as we could muster to make a fitting tribute to Cyndi as we buried her.

More courage was needed to beg Cyndi's husband to let us see our grandsons. It took courage to accept that Cyndi's husband would not allow us to see her boys. He did not want us to talk to them about Cyndi's death and declared us unfit grandparents and got a lawyer to keep us away. Not only had we lost our daughter, we lost her children as well. It has taken enormous courage to accept that we haven't seen one of Cyndi's boys for seventeen years. I now understand why some people blame anyone and everyone for the death of their loved-one. They feel that someone needs to pay the price. Even God is not exempt!

It took courage to comfort my broken-hearted husband who couldn't find words to convey his pain. It took courage to talk with our five other children about the pain of losing their sister. It took courage to speak with our eight grandchildren who couldn't comprehend that their beautiful aunt had died. And yet when the opportunity presented itself, the courage I needed seemed to appear in a way that amazed me. Courage took over after exhaustion and despair set in.

Finding the Courage to Ask for Help

Finding help when grieving is not as easy as some people think. I went to my own doctor begging for help. He responded by asking, "What kind of pill do you want?" My faith in the medical profession fell into the toilet. I went to our pastor for consolation and support. He responded that, since he knew the families of both our daughter and her husband, he couldn't take sides. "Here is the name of another priest who might help you," he suggested. My confidence in the clergy dissolved at that point.

I discovered that our church had a grief group that was open to anyone who was grieving. Some participants lost husbands, some lost parents. Losing a child is a unique grief. It took courage to go to the first meeting. The eight-week course barely touched the surface of my despair. There is a huge difference between losing your child and losing your mother. Believe me, I know.

The perfect suggestion for me became a group called, Compassionate Friends, which is an organization dedicated to parents who have lost children. I was part of that organization for seven years. Nevertheless, it took courage to go to my first meeting. Walking into a meeting with fifteen parents who are grieving is daunting at first. However, I am so glad that I did. It became my safe harbor. The one place where everyone in the room understood the depth and breadth of my grief with no judgment.

Even though Compassionate Friends helped to ease my suffering, I needed more one-on-one counseling. It took courage to sift through names and interview counselors. I dreaded telling my story to strangers. Not finding the right counselor at first is heartbreaking. Fortunately, I found the perfect counselor. I met with her for two years. Susan heard my story with an open heart and did not flinch when I told her about my transpersonal journaling. In fact, she was the first person to suggest that I write a book about my experience.

Finding the Courage to Keep Going

Courage is needed to keep the marriage together after the death of a child. Many couples divorce. Just looking at one another is a reminder of the death of your child. Our suffering felt doubled. The inability to fix the situation is painfully difficult for most men. That was true for my husband. Most women need to talk about the death. That was true for me. I have found in my own Celestial Conversation workshops that most men want to figure everything out before they talk. It becomes the elephant in the room 24/7. It takes courage, lots of prayer and patience to find ways to get the help we both needed to ease our suffering. Fortunately for me, with God's help, my husband and I were able to weather the storm of losing our child. This past year we celebrated our sixty years of marriage. We renewed our vows at Mass because we found healing in our faith.

Looking back, God gave me the courage to keep moving forward, even though I just wanted to collapse in a heap most of the time. Each day, I would try to move forward just an inch. Each day I would wake up grateful that God gave me another day to find ways to heal. The courage I needed to survive seemed to come in the nick of time. Months went by. Little by little, I found what I needed just for the day. Books were given to me that were perfect. Some friends disappeared but new friends appeared. It took courage to ignore the gossip about our daughter's suicide.

Finding Courage From the Other Side

Gradually I began to recognize that my courage had grown enough to try transpersonal journaling with our daughter, Cyndi. All my Catholic training caused me great anguish in the beginning. And yet, from the first time I journaled with Cyndi, I received exactly what I needed to begin to release my guilt about not being able to save her. In doing so, the highest investment of my courage turned out to be the most incredible healing of all.

Receiving Cyndi's words not only helped me let go of my anger, resentment and criticism of everyone involved in her death, our transpersonal journaling helped me to understand what she had been going through while she was alive. Most of which I was completely unaware of. That breakthrough inspired me to agree to have the courage to write Celestial Conversations.

Finding the Courage to Heal

Funny thing, I didn't really notice how much courage the Good Lord gave me until thirteen years later when I returned to Glastonbury. It was there I recognized my strength in revisiting where the main pain began in order to heal. And it was there that the Seven Spiritual Gifts were revealed to me.

One of the reasons I decided to share my understanding of the spiritual gifts that we receive as we walk the Grief Path in this book, is because I think I would have benefited from noticing these spiritual gifts much earlier. If I had recognized the spiritual gifts that were given to me as I walked the Grief Path, I believe my grief journey would have been easier. It is my belief, dear reader, that becoming aware of the Spiritual Gifts we receive after a loved-one dies gives us immense strength to heal our broken hearts.

Exploring Your Spiritual Gift of Courage

Here are some ideas you might find helpful as you explore your own path to courage on your spiritual grief journey:

1. **Your Courageous Decisions** - Think back to the death of your loved one and trace the courageous decisions you made from the moment you heard about his or her death. Write them down in a journal.

   - Consider the courage it took to hear the words, "Your loved one is dead." How did it affect you?
   - What did you do after that moment? Did you comfort other members of the family? Did you arrange for a funeral?
   - Reflect on the courage it took to deal with well-meaning people who said the most outrageous things. In my case, I was often

told "It's a good thing you have five other children."

- Write in your journal the situations that required your personal courage. Recall the courage it took to accept that your loved one had really died. Where did that courage come from?

2. **Your Courageous Actions** - I submit that the conscious actions that we make as a result of the death of our loved ones also demonstrate our courage. Here are a few other things to consider in your journal:

- As you moved into the new chapter of your life without your loved one, how often did you need the courage to get out of bed? Or even participate in "normal" activities like cooking, or taking a shower?
- Did you have to go back to work? Seeing your fellow employees can be very

distressing. It took courage to get dressed and return to work, let alone interact with fellow employees who knew you before the death.

- Did you seek out a grief support group? Where did you get the courage to go to that first meeting?

I encourage you to write down all the courageous actions and decisions that you can remember as you walked your grief path. Use this information as a meditation to open up to the awareness of how your soul has grown in courage.

Chapter 4
Spiritual Gift #2 - Compassion

"If your compassion does not include yourself, it is not complete."
- Buddha

Our daughter's death ripped my heart open. As a result, my compassion for other mothers who have lost a child expanded exponentially. The heartbreak of losing a child cannot be measured, but it is felt at the deepest level.

The other side of personal grief is the deep feeling of compassion for anyone who is dealing with the death of a loved one. As Daniel Goleman said, "True compassion means not only feeling another's pain, but being moved to relieve it." I felt his quote in my soul.

Sharing Compassion with Others

Recently a dear friend of mine was dying in California. I live in New Jersey and while I couldn't physically be by her bedside I wanted to do everything I could for both her and her family. I sent loving Reiki energy to her in the hospital room and shared the compassionate wisdom I had with her family.

When my friend developed Covid and was put in isolation, she was told she could no longer have any visitors. Determined that my friend not die alone, I was able to connect with Victoria, the Director of Nursing at the hospital. Victoria kindly listened to my request to allow her family to be present so they could surround her bed physically until her death. Through her own compassion,

Victoria shared that some of her own family had Covid, and had died alone in their hospital rooms in Germany. With Victoria's own compassionate help, we had the power to transform my friend's transition journey with her loving family by her side. In fact, the last text from my friend before she died was "Thank you for finding this amazing woman."

I could feel my friend's gratitude for what I was able to do before she died, and what she knows I will do for the family in the future. Even though I was 3,000 miles away, my compassion helped me join her family's loving energy as we all sent her off to heaven. Working together in that loving energy was the highest form of compassion I have ever experienced.

Funny thing, a few days after my friend's death, I called the Vice President of the hospital to congratulate that wonderful nurse who helped my friend. He said he didn't know the nurse, but he would look for her. He never found Victoria, even though I knew her name and the fact that she came from Germany just prior to covid. I believe the nurse was an angel.

Compassion for the Global Tsunami of Grief

Over the last ten years, I was given many opportunities to present my workshops all over the US. In every Celestial Conversations workshop, I met people just like me, who were hoping to receive word that their loved one was alright after the death. In many cases, the parents wanted to know that their child was able to forgive them for not saving them from death.

I felt the same way because I was in England when Cyndi died. My need to do something for the bereaved in my workshop was just as strong as my own need to find out how Cyndi died when the necessary information was withheld from me. I felt so fortunate to be able to give the broken-hearted workshop participants transpersonal journaling tools that allowed them to communicate with their deceased loved ones. It brought tears to my eyes every time that connection was made. Tears of joy.

The more Celestial Conversations workshops I gave, the more people I met who were drowning in grief. While sharing transpersonal journaling gave me great pleasure, I longed to do more. Eventually I recognized that the whole world is grieving in one way or another. As they say in the Bible, "The harvest is great, but the laborers are few." Luke 10:2

Just as my awareness of the world-wide tsunami of grief penetrated my brain, I was asked by a friend to read and endorse a book written by Daniela Norris, who lived in France. I loved her book so much that I reached out to Daniela, congratulating her on the unique way she wrote about past life regression in her novel, On Dragonfly Wings. The same week, I was asked to participate in a podcast hosted by Uma Girish, who was in the process of writing a book about the death of her mother, Losing Amma, Finding Home. These two women became my friends: Daniela, born in Israel, Uma, born in India.

We all recognized that, although we had nothing in common by way of age, culture or religion, we spoke the same language of grief. All three of us individually found a way to help others heal their grief. As we shared our stories, we co-founded The International Grief Council in 2014, which gave us a platform to speak to audiences around the United States about our personal grief experiences. This became our call to action. We decided to bring the discussion of grief out into the open. We all felt that grief as a subject was not discussed enough, no matter what country you came from. Our mutual passion made the intensity of our service to the broken-hearted multiply exponentially.

Although the coronavirus disease 2019 kept us from continuing our outreach, the need to offer our time and experience to those who were interested continues to burn brightly. The violence in our cities, the coronavirus deaths world-wide, and the war in Ukraine only added to the grief in the world. Grief is a lonely path for everyone, even if they are in a large family or have plenty of friends. Walking the trail of grief takes strength and courage and persistence. Talking about our grief is therapeutic, especially for women. Healing requires the hope that the broken-hearted person will be able to fully participate in life again. Sometimes that is all we hope for. For me the opportunity to bring hope to others has become my heart's burning desire.

Shared Compassion in our DNA

For those of us trying to survive the loss of our loved ones, compassion seeps into our DNA. Somehow it helps us to know that we are not the only individuals suffering. By turning our attention to others, helping those who need a shoulder to cry on or giving them a listening ear, we get stronger.

As I reflected on the treasures that changed me at a soul level, I thought of leaders in the grief world who used their gifts to make the world a better place. Each one seemed to have grown into their purpose because of the loss of their loved-one. They set a high bar for those of us who want to do the same:

Simon Stephens founded Compassionate Friends in England in 1969 by putting two grieving families together for mutual support. Stephen's compassion as a minister sparked an organization that has grown exponentially. I spent seven years receiving the loving support of a Compassionate Friends Chapter in New Jersey after Cyndi died. There are now over 600 chapters of Compassionate Friends in the United States and many Chapters in Europe and as far away as Australia.

Candace Lightner founded Mothers Against Drunk Driving in 1980. Her courage, after her daughter had been killed by a drunk driver, became a crusading force for tough new drinking and driving laws in the United States, establishing over 400 chapters of MADD throughout the world. She encourages everyone to take action in areas that they know need to be changed.

Dr. Gloria Horsley and Dr. Heidi Horsley founded Open to Hope in 2005. Their mission is to help people find hope after loss. As a result of the loss of Gloria's son, Scott, Open to Hope has become an international organization which helps thousands of broken-hearted individuals find healing, through conferences, podcasts, articles and television programs. Together Gloria and Heidi found a way to make a difference for others that became an international life-line for individuals who are dealing with the death of their loved-one. Their compassion for the broken-hearted sets a very high bar for every organization that reaches out to the grief-stricken.

Elizabeth Boisson and Mark Ireland founded Helping Parents Heal in 2012. Elizabeth lost 2 children. Mark lost a son. Together they co-founded this wonderful organization which allows open discussion of spiritual experiences and afterlife evidence about connecting to our deceased children. I am in awe of their work. I wish Helping Parents Heal had been available for me when Cyndi died. Some organizations do not feel comfortable discussing afterlife experiences with our deceased children, but Helping Parents Heal does allow this discussion in a non-dogmatic way. They have a facebook page and Instagram, in case you can't find a chapter near you.

Exploring Your Spiritual Gift of Compassion

No matter where you are on your grief journey, I encourage you to take a gentle look back at what you've learned on your path of grief. To help you see the progress that you've already made on your journey, and to offer some thoughts on how to continue from here, ask yourself these questions for ways you might share your gift of compassion with others.

- Is it possible that because of your experience, you now have a deeper compassion for your fellow man? How has this changed?
- If you have lost a child, does your heart ache with complete understanding when you see

the faces of the parents who may have lost a child through sickness, addiction or an accident?

- If you have lost a loved one, how does the common thread of loss and grief connect you?

- What things helped you get through your grief that you might share with them?

- What potential role can you play that will utilize your Spiritual Gift of compassion in a way that could help another feel less alone on their journey?

- Can you reach out to people you may not know who have suffered a loss, just to let them know that there is hope?

- Can you actively participate in a grief group long after you need the help yourself?

- Can you contribute to organizations that provide support during traumatic events, like the Red Cross or St. Jude's hospital?

Compassion knows no boundaries! Compassion activates you. It changes your perspective. It softens your heart. It is a spiritual gift you can only know fully from experiencing it yourself.

Chapter 5
Spiritual Gift #3 - Faith

"Faith is different from proof; the latter is human, the former is a Gift from God"
- Blaise Pascal

I believe that faith comes to us as a grace, often through the intercession of others, especially while we are grieving. Some of us lose our faith as we grieve but it is never far away. I believe that our soul keeps us connected to our Creator, even when we are furious about the circumstances or terrified of God.

Faith as a Foundation

My mother was a woman of faith. Her faith was wrapped in the fear of God, as were so many Catholics who learned about their faith prior to Vatican II. I was taught the same kind of fear-based Catholicism. As I grew older, I discovered a kinder, much gentler God in my Catholic faith that warmed my heart.

I had the good fortune to meet and get to know Archbishop Fulton Sheen in the early nineteen seventies. He gave me a new opportunity to see and understand the love of God through Jesus Christ. Sheen's book, The Life of Christ, inspired me to begin to comprehend the incredible agape-love that Christ has for His children. When I read Sheen's book, I was just beginning to understand the deep love a parent had for his/her children because I had five children of my own. It blew me away to think that God would send His only son to

Earth to suffer and die for the sins of many. As a human being, I couldn't comprehend that kind of love. Parents all over the world lay down their lives for their children. Yet I couldn't comprehend a parent asking their child to die for a Cause…. any Cause.

I have read about Muslims asking a child to carry a bomb into a synagogue or hotel or an army base. I've read about parents offering up their child to be sacrificed, as the Indians did in Mexico centuries ago. I've read of people offering up their child to the convent or Buddhist monks to be raised by others as a gift to their God. I just can't imagine considering such a thing.

In my own life I have had the good fortune of feeling God's presence from the time I was a child. I've had the blessing of turning to God when I felt lost and alone. My parents divorced when I was twelve. I felt that God held my hand when my parents didn't or couldn't. I felt God's presence every time I gazed at the angelic face of each of my six children. I often thought of how challenging it must have been for Mary, the mother of Christ, as she went through her trials raising Jesus. I was especially helped by Mary's example when our daughter, Cyndi, died. I went to the Holy Land to walk the Via Dolorosa in Jerusalem and soak in the peace of Galilee. I never felt closer to God than in those days. This trip taught me how many of our great spiritual leaders endured the grief of losing their child.

Putting Faith to the Test

Faith is like a muscle of the body. It needs to be exercised. My faith has been tested many times, but never so much as when our daughter died. The concept of your child's death is never really contemplated by parents, prior to a severe diagnosis or death. Most parents feel as Rose Kennedy stated when President Jack Kennedy was killed, "It's not natural for a parent to bury their child." Parents expect to die first. I certainly felt that way.

When Cyndi died, I found the local priest less than helpful, so I turned to God directly for help and guidance. I was fortunate that at no time during my grief did I blame God for Cyndi's death. I pictured God welcoming her home. As in the story of the Prodigal Son in the New Testament, the father runs out to meet his errant son and welcomes him home. I pictured Cyndi being welcomed in the same manner when she died. It comforted me to know that Our heavenly Father was helping me to see that His love would dry her tears and heal her broken heart.

As I continued my Transpersonal Journaling with my mother and daughter after Cyndi's death, they both confirmed the loving way that Cyndi was welcomed into the world beyond the veil. My mother and my husband Ray's brother, Arthur, died prior to Cyndi's passing. Nevertheless, Cyndi wrote the following transpersonal note in my journal about her own death:

"I fell into bed and all of a sudden Grandma was there with Uncle Artie. I was so happy to see Uncle Artie. He made me smile. I wasn't exhausted anymore. We just sat and talked. I talked and Grandma was there. Uncle Artie kept asking me questions about the family. Much later I noticed we weren't in my bedroom anymore. I realized that Uncle Artie and Grandma were dead. I began to realize that I was dead ………." Cyndi Idleman pg 70 Celestial Conversations: Healing Relationships After Death.

Faith in the After-Life

I read that deceased family members came to visit the dying when I was a hospice volunteer. I listened to hospice personnel witnessing the conversations and/or images of deceased family members interacting with patients who were passing in front of their eyes. Cyndi's transpersonal message was so comforting to me. She shared how being with her grandmother and uncle made her transition so much easier.

Years ago, while visiting a friend, she told me that her mother had just come to visit a few minutes before I arrived in her hospital room. My friend was 75 and her mother was long dead. As my friend described the conversation with her mother, her face was filled with joy. I didn't doubt that she had a visit from her deceased mother. Over my years, as a hospice volunteer, I learned that many patients spoke of visits from the other side of the veil. Both my own mother and Cyndi opened my mind to the fact that visits from those who have died are not just possible, they are probable.

Cyndi's account amazed me. My daughter shared what happened AS SHE DIED. You can't imagine my relief after reading Cyndi's words. She was not alone in her bed with no one in the house as I pictured her. Her two favorite people came to take her home. My mother's Transpersonal Journaling helped even more:

> "Dear, dear Loanne, I am here with Cyndi. She is fine. Surprised but fine. I am with her, helping with her process, loving her and loving you." (Lois Janes, pg. 50 *Celestial Conversations: Healing Relationships After Death.)*

Tearfully, I accepted both accounts as fact, even though I didn't understand—my Catholic faith told me this was impossible—and I knew neither my mother nor my daughter would lie to me under the circumstances. After reading the transpersonal notes, I felt grateful—more centered than I'd been since I first heard about Cyndi's death.

Rediscovering a Renewed Faith

Like the mustard seed of Christ's teaching, my faith grew enormously over the next few months. My heart felt the loving Christ caring for my daughter and for me. I felt angels beside me in ways that had not happened since I was a child. My overwhelming sadness mixed with hope and extraordinary gratitude for the love of God. When I went to church, I felt God's presence deeply. His comfort filled my soul. I knew Cyndi was in good hands.

My faith grew exponentially when my brother escorted me to the Holy Land in 2007. I found the experience deeply moving and highly educational. I never realized how many of God's special people from the Old and New Testament had lost children. I discovered that the lives of David and Mary shared common grief over the loss of a child. The Western Wall, known as the Wailing Wall, is a powerful tribute to the millions of individuals, regardless of their religious faith, who pray to God to help them through their grief.

My grown-up faith continues to this day. I wake up asking God "How can I serve?" I find that each day something or someone comes into my life giving me an opportunity to be of service. As Louise Hay used to say, "What you focus on grows." My focus is serving God by helping others who have walked the Path of Grief as I have. My intention to be of service fills my life with individuals growing from their grief. It has been said that the 'harvest is great, and the workers are few.' I love working on this harvest. Helping individuals who have lost their child helps me heal my own broken heart and warms my soul.

In the process my faith has expanded to appreciate the many ways human beings reach up to their God. Whether they be of a different faith or no organized religion, I appreciate the thirst for spirituality that seems to be spreading across the planet, especially since the Covid pandemic has isolated so many of us. Solitude seems to make us look up for guidance. Many different religious faiths look up to something more. Some call it God. Some call it Heavenly Father as I do. I feel so grateful that God reaches down to us and walks with us through thick and through thin.

Exploring Your Spiritual Gift of Faith

Sometimes the best way of reinforcing our faith is to take a look at all the times our faith has been with us walking beside us through our grief. Faith can come through many things. Here are a few powerful building blocks to look for that can help you find and strengthen your spiritual gift of faith.

- **Power of a Support:** Are people who have prayed for you, supported you on your path of grief that have given you the chance to consider your own faith in God or a higher power? Who are they and what did they do for you?

- **Power of Prayer:** Is there someone you knew who prayed for you as you moved through your grief? Perhaps they prayed when you couldn't pray. What did knowing that those prayers were being sent your way mean to you?

- **Power of Reflection:** Perhaps witnessing the faith of others reminded you to consider the meaning of your own life. Or the sharing in another's grief story helped you know that you are not alone.

- **Power of Grace:** Sometimes the path of faith means releasing control. It can take the form of knowing that your healing will come in its own time and in its own way. Being kind to yourself knowing that all the answers that you seek will come. And that with faith, wisdom and grace will follow.

I believe these opportunities were presented to you to help you remember that Faith is a gift freely given by God for us to use throughout our lives, but most importantly when we are suffering. Consider asking God to give you a sign of His Love. There is no treasure on earth that can compare with the awareness of God wrapping you in His Love. That is faith in the unconditional love that is there for you always.

Chapter 6
Spiritual Gift #4 - Spiritual Expansion

"It's not in the stars to hold our destiny,
but in ourselves"
- William Shakespeare

After Cyndi died, I felt enormous guilt that I couldn't prevent her death. I prayed to Mary, the Mother of Christ. Her presence and rosary gave me great solace, especially in the middle of the night. I could picture her on the Via Dolorosa in Jerusalem witnessing her Son's desolate condition as He carried His cross to Golgotha. I often whispered, "How did you do it Mary? How did you survive the excruciating death of your child?" More to the point, "How did you go on after His death?"

Lo Anne Mayer

While I continued to prayerfully ask for help from Mother Mary, little did I know that her answer would come to me through an unexpected trip to her homeland.

On a Wing and a Prayer

When my brother mentioned that he had just come back from the Holy Land, I asked him if he would take me the next time he traveled there. Jack's answer was immediate. "Do you really want to go?" My reply was equally prompt. "Yes, Yes and Yes!" We set a date to travel on February 24, 2007. Before I knew it, I was on an airplane flying to the Holy Land.

Jack and I checked into the El Al Hotel in Jerusalem, and quickly sat down for dinner to plan our visits to the Holy Sites. Almost everything I wanted to see was inside the wall around the city.

Jerusalem is only one-third of a mile square, but it houses three religions: Christians, Muslims and Jews. We planned to start our site-seeing early the next morning.

At 8:00 am we walked from the hotel to the West Gate. The size of the wall around Jerusalem is enormous! It is almost forty feet high and over eight feet thick. My own 5'2" stature made me feel like a caterpillar as we climbed the path to the Damascus Gate. We walked directly to the Church of the Holy Sepulcher, ignoring the vendors along the way. My eyes were barely adjusting to the darkness inside the church when I looked down and saw the burial slab of Jesus Christ in front of me. My knees buckled. Tears fell from my eyes. This marked the exact spot where Jesus was brought down from the cross into Mary's arms. I could hardly breathe, as I knelt there. I was also vividly reminded that I never got to hold my own dead daughter. She was already in the casket when I came home from England.

Someone whispered that one could touch the place where Christ's cross was inserted in the ground if I went upstairs. Without saying a word, I raced up the stairs to take my place in line and waited for my turn to touch the base of the cross of Christ. Truly an out-of-body experience for me. His death was so real at that moment, and death was the reason I was here.

Hundreds of people filled the area around the burial slab as I came down the stairs. Jack led me about 100 feet further to the left in this huge church into The Little House. Tradition says that this was the tomb of Christ where He lay for three days. Jack and I didn't speak. There were no words. I knelt to say my heartfelt prayer: "Before I die, Lord, I need to be able to forgive anyone who might have been involved in the death of my daughter."

When I came out of the quiet Little House, even more people filled the Church of the Holy Sepulcher. In reaching for Jack to grab his hand, I bumped into a visiting American priest from a town near me in New Jersey. He was waiting his turn to be part of the procession of the Catholic priests to celebrate Mass. I asked if he would celebrate Mass for Cyndi. When he agreed to do so, I felt my prayers were being answered. What were the odds of meeting an American priest from my home state who was stationed at the Church of the Holy Sepulcher who was willing to celebrate Mass for Cyndi?

A Spiritual Breakthrough

By now the immense crowd of tourists was making it impossible to move. We walked down to the Wailing Wall, also known as the Western Wall or Solomon's Wall. This is the most sacred site for the

Jewish people. My eyes zeroed in on one solitary woman holding her daughter about the age of three. The little girl's golden blonde hair reminded me of Cyndi at that age. As her mother placed her hand on the women's side of the wall, she became a vision of prayer and meditation before my eyes. Jewish devotions believe that "the Divine Presence never departs from the Western Wall."

I felt her devotion as I walked down to the women's side of the wall and placed pieces of paper, with written prayer requests given to me by friends, inside the wall's crevices.

I added my own prayer to learn forgiveness. As I look back, this is where my breakthrough to forgiveness began.

Jack and I moved on to The Tower of David Museum, which now offers an exhibition devoted to the history of Jerusalem. I was acutely aware that David had lost one son. I didn't realize that he lost three sons. We watched a movie about King David's many accomplishments. I learned that he had not only recovered from the loss of his children, but he defeated his countries' enemies and brought peace to Israel. He then anointed his son, Solomon, as the King of Israel. It suddenly gave me hope that my life was not over and I could rise above the sadness of our daughter's death. Rain forced us to leave the fortress. We ducked into King David's tomb and The Cenacle. I sucked in my breath as I literally felt David's presence. This was a man who was not overcome by his grief. He went on to live a purposeful life.

Another Past Life Remembered

The next day we drove to Quamrun which drew me in the minute we walked through the entrance. The hills beyond were 600 ft. high which held the caves where the Essenes lived over 2,000 years ago. The Essenes were a separatist group of Jews who participated in the first Jewish revolt against Rome. I felt keenly that I knew what those caves looked like. I didn't need to explore them. I walked directly to one of the in-ground baths and was immediately thrust into a past-life experience. A voice deep inside me said. "You lived here. This is where you learned to judge other people." The truth of that statement rang throughout my whole body.

In my reverie, I could also see a man coming up the ladder out of the deep bath in front of me. He didn't look like me, but I knew the man who emerged from the water was me. I watched the ghost of my past put on a white robe and kneel to pray. He had just finished a penitential ritual bath to release his judgment. Finishing his prayer, he walked right past me toward the communal meal. It was so real I could have reached out to touch him. "What does this mean?" I wondered. How do I release my judgment of those who I believed influenced Cyndi's death?

Jack found me. "It is hot. Let's go swimming in the Dead Sea!" he chirped. We set off for a beach nearby. We both love to swim but the black, wet clay that led to the water did not entice me. Jack headed for the water. I sat in a beach chair reminiscing about my past-life experience in Quamrun. Collective judgment can destroy whole communities. The Essenes were peace-loving, but that conviction did not prevent them from going to war against Rome. That decision destroyed them completely. I resolved to release my judgment.... but how?

Gethsemane, Galilee and Understanding Purpose

We moved onto the Garden of Gethsemane. So beautiful. So painful. The eight olive trees seemed to hold the tears of millions of visitors, as well as those of Jesus Christ. The garden is small but filled with roses and daisies, hibiscus and irises. All lovingly cared for by the Franciscans. I prayed for help to use the grief I was enduring to make a positive difference in the world. There was a Mass going on at the Basilica of the Agony. It was the perfect ending to that visit.

I wanted to see Mt Carmel on the way to Galilee, but we never found it. We didn't realize that Mt. Carmel is a mountain range that is four to five miles wide and 1,791 feet high. I was acutely aware from my biblical studies that Elijah had a famous contest with the 450 prophets of Baal to decide whose deity was in control of Israel. I knew that the Carmelites founded their Catholic order on Mt. Carmel. I had been friendly with our Carmelite sisters in NJ for over forty years. I wanted to tell them that I found Mt. Carmel. The whole time we were searching I could feel a familiar energy, but I thought we were looking for a town, not a mountain. How many times in my life have I searched for something that was right under my nose?

On the northwestern side of the Sea of Galilee, we came to the Mount of the Beatitudes, with its bougainvillea, lilies, poppies and gladiolas. Jack and I could hear a choir in the eight-sided small chapel singing Amazing Grace in Chinese. As we walked on the portico outside the chapel, I remembered that I had a picture of my friend, Archbishop Fulton Sheen, taken in this very spot. The Mount of the Beatitudes was my favorite spot in Galilee but the only thing I bought in the gift shop was a copy of the Sermon on the Mount. The one sentence "Blessed are those who mourn, for they will be comforted" really seared my soul. That plaque still hangs in my office as a reminder of the comfort I have received from the Good Lord.

Returning to Jerusalem Jack went to have lunch with a New York Times reporter he knew. I went to the Via Dolorosa to walk the Stations of the Cross. I joined a German Group at El Omarlyck College which was where the Stations began on the Via

Dolorosa. I watched a mother and father carry their daughter in a wheelchair up the many steps as we proceeded through the streets of Jerusalem. Their devotion to their child morphed into my commitment to carry my own dead child's memory with purpose and dedication.

Walking in the Footsteps of Christ

When Jack met me back at the hotel, he was full of enthusiasm. He had found a way to grant my most heartfelt request. He said, "Be ready to go to Bethlehem tomorrow at 8:00 am." As we drove to the Church of the Nativity, we couldn't help but notice the twenty-five-foot wall looming like a monster right next to the road. As we entered the church, we had to walk carefully around the construction that was going on until we found the stairwell leading down to the altar downstairs. There was so much incense coming up from the lower floor that we could hardly see the steps.

Once the incense cleared, we saw an altar with a fourteen-pointed star about twenty inches in diameter beneath it.

This marked the spot where Christ was believed to be born. I immediately knelt to kiss the star and say a prayer of thanksgiving for everyone who brought me to this sacred place. I knew that I would always be grateful for the chance to go to Bethlehem. It still warms my heart, especially on Christmas morning.

When we got back to Jerusalem, Jack and I walked one last time to the center of Jerusalem. As we looked toward the Western Wall, we met a wonderful British man who took the picture of us that sits on my desk today as a reminder of the amazing journey my brother and I shared. This trip cemented in my mind how many of God's people went through excruciating times but came through their difficulties by turning to God. Without a doubt my faith in God was stronger than ever because of this trip. I know with absolute certainty that God cares for me individually, as He does for you.

This trip gave me a glimpse of the Treasures in Grief. Clearly my own Gift of Faith grew enormously during this adventure. When I returned home, saying the rosary was more vivid and my experience of going to Mass seemed to transport me back to the Holy Land on a weekly basis. I recognized that I had been given a glimpse of the universal grief and an introduction to the heroes who had not only endured grief but used their grief as a reason to give back to others. I prayed that being part of this fraternity of the broken-hearted might be the catalyst for me to help the world become a better place.

Exploring Your Spiritual Gift of Spiritual Expansion

Spiritual expansion is about looking at your grief through the lens of what it has taught you about your life and reason for being here. For many, it can be difficult to see your grief as expanding your spirit in any way, and yet if we are open to looking at ourselves as spirits having a human experience, there can be no doubt that this has offered you many spiritual lessons along the way.

Here are a few practices that might help you identify and amplify your own spiritual expansion.

1. **Prayerful Meditation** - Whenever I am in doubt, need to find meaning or guidance, I sit down quietly and ask for help. You don't need to know how to meditate specifically, just take a few minutes in a quiet space. Close your eyes and set your intention for divine loving guidance

to come through. If you feel comfortable doing so, write out anything that comes to you. You might be surprised how much wisdom and insight you receive, especially if you make this a regular practice.

2. **Find your Spirit Space** - What places inspire you? You don't have to jump on an airplane to achieve spiritual enlightenment. Go to a park, beach or backyard that makes you feel connected to the earth. Feel your presence and impact upon it and the people in your life. Take stock of who you are and the incredible spirit that you are who has had the courage to take on this life journey and all you have learned along the way.

3. **Play Your Life Movie** - This is a wonderful way to replay your life from a new perspective. Pretend you are in the audience watching the movie of your life unfold. How have you changed? How has your spiritual life expanded?

What is the "spirit" of you? How do you want the movie to end?

As you play with these practices, allow yourself to be judgment free, knowing that you are always doing the best that you can. Your spiritual expansion is not about "shoulds" or "expectation," it's about letting yourself grieve and grow in whatever way feels right for you.

Chapter 7
Spiritual Gift #5 – Forgiveness

"You who want peace can only find it by complete forgiveness"

- A Course in Miracles

Raised as a pre-Vatican II Catholic, I was taught that the word forgiveness required going to confession and receiving absolution from a priest. Until I was forty years old, I don't recall ever having a conversation about forgiveness or even thinking that forgiving someone would be good for my own health and wellbeing.

What Louise Hay Taught Me

Enter Louise Hay, whom I met in 1989 at a conference in California. Louise had written an amazing book, You Can Heal Your Life, which came into my hands when my life was overwhelmingly chaotic. Reading her simple, direct words about the importance of forgiveness as a gift to myself spoke to my heart. I had huge resentment towards a long list of people, and I had no idea how to release it. The decision in 1989 to go to Louise Hay's conference in Lake Arrowhead, California, completely changed my life!

Louise taught that "The road to freedom is through the doorway of forgiveness." She went on to say, "We may not know how to forgive, and we may not want to forgive, but if we are willing to forgive, we may begin the healing process. It is imperative for our own healing that we release the past and forgive everyone." Those words spoke to my heart.

I began the process of forgiveness the first day of the conference. Louise taught us to picture the person resented, while using the affirmation at least 500 times a day, "I am willing to forgive you." At first it felt too simple.

Over time and with persistence, I felt the resentment fading. I found it so effective that I became a certified Louise Hay teacher in 1996. I taught her incredible "Healing Your Life" philosophy for twelve years. Concentrating on letting go of fear, resentment, criticism and guilt which I taught in every class, I thought I had completely forgiven everyone. WRONG!

Blame and Judgment Sabotages Forgiveness

The challenges of having a big family have given me many opportunities to add to my list of people whom I judged. Even though I knew the power of forgiveness, I did not continue to focus on it after I stopped teaching Louise's course. Life got in the way: Our oldest son's marriage ended in divorce. I blamed his wife. When our daughter, Cyndi, had a son diagnosed with autism, I blamed the medical profession. When the challenge of Cyndi's marriage led to divorce, I blamed her husband. Another grandson's diagnosis of neuroblastoma at 9 months of age engaged my family in a literal fight for life that sucked the strength out of me. The death of my mother brought up all the resentments I held against her for most of my life, plus the guilt of not being able to heal our relationship before she died. I realized that I had a lot of forgiveness work to do. After Mother's death and Cyndi's officially declared suicide, I decided to return to forgiveness as a daily exercise.

Lo Anne Mayer

Another Past Life Vision and an Opportunity to Learn Forgiveness

The Universe provided me with an unusual teacher. Enter my co-founder of the International Grief Council, Daniela Norris. Together with our co-founder, Uma Girish, we decided to offer a retreat at Charney Manor in England. During that retreat, Daniela, who is now a certified Past Life Regressionist, offered a group past-life experience. I was excited to participate. I didn't know much about past life regression at the time. In the process of our group regression, I dropped into a farm in the Midwest of the U.S. in the 1800s. I was happily married with a daughter but had no other extended family. In this past-life regression, my husband had gone hunting for game. My little girl and I were in the cornfields when a group of marauders came into the property, ransacked our house, took our livestock and burned all the buildings to the ground. They rode off without ever seeing my daughter and me hiding in the cornfield.

In my past-life regression, after 24 hours of crying and hiding in the cornfield, my daughter and I heard a single horse riding into our property. Peeking out cautiously, we saw a stranger with a dead man slung over his horse coming to a stop as he stared at the burnt down buildings. Looking around, he got off his horse. My daughter and I came out of the cornfield feeling that he might help us. I immediately recognized that the rider was Cyndi's husband in my present life. The person I blamed the most for Cyndi's death. Completely shocked and surprised, I froze in my seat at Charney Manor as the past life regression continued.

The stranger explained how he found my husband dying from a gunshot wound. He tried to save him without success. My husband of the 1890's begged this stranger to take him home, which was the reason for his sad visit. Looking around at the devastation of our farm, the stranger softly said, "Let me help you." In that past life regression, the stranger stayed to help me rebuild and eventually we fell in love, married and had a long and happy life together. The past life experience softened my anger and judgment against Cyndi's husband in this life. It opened my eyes, once again, to the power of forgiveness.

Since that experience I have found that every time I think of Cyndi's husband, I think of him riding into my property in the 1800's and all the help he gave me to rebuild my life. Forgiving him for his role in Cyndi's death in my present life has become so much easier. It is as if my lack of forgiveness melted like a snowman on a warm Spring Day.

This experience also reminded me of all the transpersonal journaling messages from my mother and my daughter that contained the admonition, FORGIVE. On page 54 of Celestial Conversations: Healing Relationships After Death, I reread my mother's words "Forgiveness is the balm. Do not be distracted by blame or anger. Choose the forgiveness road no matter what your mind tells you. Teach by example. There is no other way." How could I have forgotten her wise words?

This experience also gave me the clear impression of what forgiveness does to my own body, mind and spirit. The people that I have held responsible for hurting me, whether it be a teacher who didn't help me or a colleague that criticized me or someone in politics who infuriates me, I must remember that it is my own choice to forgive. At least I must be at least willing to do so. If the willingness to forgive seems too difficult, Louise Hay encouraged us to use this affirmation: "I am willing to be willing to forgive." Sometimes I had to affirm "I am willing to be willing to be willing to forgive." I had to back the affirmation as far as necessary to speak the affirmation honestly.

The Lifelong Process of Forgiveness

When I look over my own life, I realize that forgiveness is an ongoing process. I shall never finish the list. Life is full of opportunities to judge or criticize.

So now, many years after Cyndi's death I continue to make a list of those who I have yet to forgive. Like dust that settles in the crevices of a home, lack of forgiveness seeps into the crevices of our mind and body. To be truly healed, I can't hold back my forgiveness. I must begin again and again. I recognize Cyndi's words to me in our transpersonal journaling were the truth. "Don't waste time, Mom. You don't have it to waste. Look for the light. You are on the right path. Forgiveness is the key. The key to God's world, which is truly wonderful." Cyndi

Idleman pg 72 Celestial Conversations: Healing Relationships After Death.

When I first read Cyndi's transpersonal letter to me in my journal, I was more than surprised. She wasn't much of a religious person in her life on earth. She held many judgments against her husband, the medical profession and the educational system. Reading her words "Forgiveness is the key" really caused me to stop and ponder. I asked my mother and Cyndi in our transpersonal journaling to help me understand Karma. They both replied that our Karma depends on forgiving while we were alive. The price of not forgiving means that we get to come back in our next life to be with the people we couldn't forgive in this life. Do it now or do it later is the law of the Universe. That gave me even more incentive to find my way to forgiveness. Now I am much more prone to act on forgiveness than on resentment.

Exploring Your Spiritual Gift of Forgiveness

My hope is that you will find your own way, dear reader, to forgive those who have hurt you. Letting go is a challenge but well worth the trouble.

1. **Write a Forgiveness List:** Having a tool handy to use when forgiveness is needed is like having the key to the lock in your door. You might want to add this little exercise that I use quite often:

   - Take a piece of paper and make a list of all the people you believe you need to forgive.
   - Then fold the paper in half lengthwise. Turn the paper to the clean side and make a list of those people who need to forgive you.
   - Open up the full page. Notice how many names are the same on both lists.
   - The takeaway: Those we choose to forgive are those who need to forgive us for

whatever we did in response to their negativity.

2. **Forgiveness Affirmations**: I highly recommend using Louise Hay's words of affirmation 500 times a day for thirty days. It could make all the difference for you:

> "I am willing to forgive you, (name the person specifically) for not being the person I wanted you to be. I forgive you and I set you free."

It can be very effective if you visualize that person as if you were speaking directly to his/her face to face. Even better if you have a picture. Try this at first on someone who hurt you in a minor way to feel the effectiveness of this process. Then try it with someone more intensely hurtful. You will be surprised how automatic this forgiveness formula can be! I have learned to do this regularly so the resentment doesn't settle into my body. The secret, of course, is to simply do it!

Perhaps you have learned other ways to forgive. Whatever process of forgiveness that is working for you is one of the Gifts of Grief that God has given you. Welcome it! Use it! Be Grateful for it!

Chapter 8
Spiritual Gift #6 – Unconditional Love

"Forgive everyone as quickly as you can. Make it your primary purpose of each day. Forgiveness is the key to the door of unconditional love."

- Lois Janes Celestial Conversations: Healing Relationships After Death (p.37)

Having only known conditional love my whole life long, I found my mother's advice in her quote above rather ironic. This advice stopped me cold as I was connecting with her transpersonally. She had always seemed conditional to me. "Do this and I will be proud of you." "Achieve that and I will really be happy." However, as we conversed through our transpersonal journaling after her death, her loving words were clearly unconditional.

She wasn't the only source of conditional love in my childhood. I went to Catholic schools and my Catholic religion in the fifties was very conditional. "If you lie, God will not forgive you, unless you confess your sin." As a child I took that to mean that God wouldn't love me anymore period. Some priests even said as much, or at least that was what my seven-year-old mind understood. The nuns were even more creative when they taught us that God cried every time we committed a sin.

Conditional Love was a large part of living in my military family. My father's West Point training trickled down to conditional living. Living on military bases meant there were rules for everything, such as: "You may not play with non-commissioned officers' children," being a prime example of what was expected. Good grades, good children, strict bedtime, don't touch my uniform, etc.

The Real Meaning of Unconditional Love

Unconditional love was introduced to me as an adult as my Catholic faith evolved into teaching about a kinder, gentler God. Even though I understood the philosophy, I did not include it in my own life as much as I might have. I was a conditional mother as taught by my own conditional parents.

Now that I have a dead daughter to reflect upon, I recognize how much unconditional love could have changed my relationship with Cyndi. I deeply regret not understanding how unconditional love could have been a major part of my life before Cyndi died. In fact, it might have saved her life.

My husband, Ray, is the epitome of unconditional love. He has always been able to understand and articulate each side of any difficulty. He listens and ponders his advice before he speaks. His gentle prodding usually helps everyone in our family come to their own conclusions. It has been a learning experience to watch him deal with the many hills and valleys of our married life with loving understanding. He often articulates ways to help me see the possibilities of solving a situation without any conditions, just suggestions that will help me choose. I have learned most of my comprehension of unconditional love from him. Knowing that you are loved unconditionally is the best gift anyone can give to another human being.

The experience of being "loved anyway," as Mother Teresa so beautifully expresses, is so comforting to every human being. Unconditional love without the need for explanation or conversation has been one of my husband's biggest gifts to me. It brought me deeper and deeper in love with him. I can honestly say that Ray's unconditional love was the secret to our sixty years of marriage.

Unconditional Loving Compassion

After Cyndi's death, I became much more unconditional in my love for everyone. I began to see clearly the exquisite pain of parents who lost their child. Even if the parent contributed to the death of their child by denial or ignorance, I could feel my heart going out to them. The more I meet the broken-hearted through my workshops, the more compassion I have for those who are grieving. The more compassion I developed, the more unconditional I became.

The first time I noticed my own unrestricted unconditional love for another after Cyndi died happened in 2007. My friend, Susan, lost her husband after a long, protracted illness. Susan is also a Reiki Master. We often drove to Reiki meetings together and shared Reiki with each other. She had even traveled to England with me to go to Glastonbury and on to our Grief Retreat in Charney Manor. I felt we had forged a solid friendship.

Years after our trip to England, Susan's husband died. I offered to help her in any way when he died and on many subsequent occasions. Finally, I realized that Susan didn't want my help. Nor did she want my presence in any form. Surprised and saddened by her reaction, I recognized that she was going through grief in her own way.

My reaction was total unconditional love for her. I sent Reiki to her, prayed for her journey and backed off for as long as it took for her to find her balance. Having been through my own grief, I was certain that Susan would find her way back to our friendship. Five years later that has not occurred, but when I think of her I do so with total unconditional love. She is my friend and she is finding her way as a chaplain for a hospital nearby. I am certain that she is bringing peace and understanding to each of her patients. Though I miss her friendship, I still cherish the memories we shared together.

Unconditional Loving Acceptance

Those who are experiencing grief for any reason, whether it be the loss of a loved-one, the loss of a job, the loss of a pet or property need unconditional love as they try to put their lives together. So often we try to fix people or tell them what they should do when all they want is to be heard and/or hugged.

Unconditional love allows people to be where they are. No pressure. That can be especially true of people who are experiencing anticipatory grief as they witness the loss of a loved one to cancer or any life-threatening disease. Unconditional love is the exact medicine we all need and yet so many of us have no clue how to offer it to those in need.

Unconditional Love of Self

The hardest part of learning unconditional love for me was applying it to myself. Many parents, including me, blame themselves for not being able to save their child from death. That can be true of anyone who lost a loved-one and was helpless to stop their death.

Cyndi told me in our transpersonal journaling, "There is nothing that you could have done to save me from my path of self-destruction." Pg 71 Celestial Conversations: Healing Relationships After Death. Despite that, I still played the shoulda-woulda-coulda-game for years. I would wonder, 'What If I had not been in England when she died? What could I have noticed about her situation that would have alerted me to her potential death?' It is normal for a parent to second-guess what he/she might have done to save their child.

It took years for me to practice unconditional love for myself, in spite of the fact that I taught Louise Hay's Healing Your Life Course for twelve years, with particular emphasis on "loving yourself." Even then I still hadn't incorporated unconditional love into my own persona. It is something that you, dear reader, could consider. Unconditional love is the healing balm for your broken heart. The trickle-down effect for those of us who grieve is that we can more readily see the weaknesses in all human beings. It seems that tears wash away the blinders from our eyes. Grief helps us to see everyone as doing the very best they can. Heartbreak makes us less judgmental.

The treasure in this awareness is that we recognize that all of us are human beings. All of us, whether kings or immigrants, mourn the death of someone we love. All of us need help to recover from loss. Unconditional love is the key to softening the pain and letting someone find their own way.

Unconditional Love from a New Perspective

As Cyndi expressed to me in one of my transpersonal journals, "From my new perspective, none of it matters because we all do the best that we can, even those of us who appear to fail. There is no failure in heaven, even though there is no heaven as we thought. There is just love." Pg. 72 Celestial Conversations: Healing Relationships After Death.

I have grown gradually into unconditional love. More and more I look at individuals, situations, even strangers with a loving intent. The more I release my own judgment, the more I see with eyes of love. The more I release criticism of the individual or situation, the easier I can see what's underneath their perspective, their bravado, their thirst for loving understanding. It is as if God removed the barriers to my understanding in order to see that the person in front of me just needs my unconditional love. Sometimes that means I just smile and listen to their story .

Exploring Your Spiritual Gift of Unconditional Love

The greatest treasure in our Gifts from Grief, is learning how to incorporate unconditional love into our lives. This is truly the diamond in our treasure chest. All other gifts flow from this one gift. Here is how you can incorporate all of these spiritual gifts in this way.

1. **Spiritual Gift #1 - Courage:** Practicing courage with unconditional love makes your courage a gift to all.

2. **Spiritual Gift #2 - Compassion:** Practicing compassion with unconditional love gives those who witness your humble approach to life a reminder of Jesus Christ.

3. **Spiritual Gift #3 - Faith:** Your faith, practiced with unconditional love gives onlookers a taste of our heavenly Father.

4. **Spiritual Gift #4 - Spiritual Expansion:** Your spiritual expansion practiced with unconditional love gives those who admire you the inspiration to explore spirituality themselves.

5. **Spiritual Gift #5 - Forgiveness:** If you practice forgiveness with unconditional love you show the world how to live in this divisive time.

6. **Spiritual Gift #6 - Unconditional Love:** If your purpose is wrapped in unconditional love, to paraphrase Mother Teresa, 'You will do something beautiful for God.'

All of this wrapped together prepares you for your final spiritual gift, Mission.

Chapter 9
Spiritual Gift #7 – Mission

"Make your life a mission – not an intermission"
- Arnold H. Glasgow. American Psychologist

Our lives are made up of many purposes. From the time we are very young, our purpose is determined by our surroundings. If you were a poor child, you may have decided that your purpose would be to create a life where you have enough money that you never have to worry about finances. Because of a childhood trauma, you may have decided to create a life where you would never feel afraid again. It could be, as was my childhood purpose, to do whatever I could to keep my mother from crying after my father asked for a divorce. I did everything I could to make her happy as much as I could. When I succeeded, I felt a visceral joy. It made me want to help others. I tried to help everyone in my small world, friends, teachers, and neighbors. Because of my mother's pain, I recognized suffering in the people around me. The word "healing" was not in my vocabulary, but my intention was to ease everyone's pain.

You might have had an incredible coach who made you believe that you could be an all-star soccer player. You may have had an uncle who was extremely successful in finance and you decided to follow in his footsteps. You might have had a next-door neighbor who ran for political office who inspired you to find a place in government. You might have discovered a large family in your neighborhood that was filled with love. They inspired you to want to have a family like that as an adult. Each expanded purpose helps flesh out the mission that, I believe, you came into this planet to complete. Most of us don't remember the mission that was planted in our soul. We just followed the threads of life.

Understanding our Earthly Mission

Before we come to Earth, I believe we plan our life with the help of God and His angels. I don't believe that we are randomly dropped onto the planet. We are purposefully given the chance to live on Earth. A chance to teach and to learn. Life is a gift from God. I have also come to believe that we know exactly what our mission is when we are born. Most of us forget by the time we are six or seven. Many little ones can still see the angels or invisible friends until they get to school. Very often the big people in our lives discourage us from sharing what we, as children, can see with our eyes. This makes some of us timid about sharing what we experience spiritually when we are young. As we grow our purpose keeps us moving toward our mission for this life. Sometimes the mission comes on the heels of a trauma.

Perhaps you have found, as I have, that your mission has unfolded in unexpected ways and for unexpected reasons. As an example, even though I taught religious education for children at our church, I had no desire to be a teacher. Along came Louise Hay, an extraordinary motivational speaker and founder of Hay House. In my opinion, she was the mother of the Mindfulness Movement. After attending one of her earliest conferences in 1988, I decided on the spot to become one of her certified teachers. Her ability to help individuals to understand and utilize the mind-body connection was so inspiring that I wanted to follow her example. It was my joy to teach Healing Your Life courses for twelve years. What you teach, you learn. Those years changed and expanded my purpose. After years of teaching children at home, n church and in scouting, I relished teaching adults.

Following the Path of Inspiration

Did you ever read a book and feel impelled to meet the author? Alma Daniel's book, Ask Your Angels, was so inspiring that I jumped at the chance to take her course in person. I was so inspired by Alma that I quickly agreed to teach her course when she gave me the invitation to do so. My purpose at that time was to help everyone get in touch with their angel. During the seven years that I taught this course, I witnessed the joy that came to others who found immense help from their angel. Of course, it also increased my communication with my own angel.

I began to see that I could help make the world a better place through teaching. I sensed a mission developing. Teaching the angel course inspired me to notice all the good that was being done by members of my own community. That awareness helped me write and produce a cable television show focusing on the wonderful people in our community who acted as angels to others. I called it "Angels at Work." With the help of my daughter, Karen, we launched an inspirational television show that focused on interviewing the people in our community who were making a positive difference. Karen and I developed a long list of individuals who were quietly making the world a better place without making the headlines. The purpose of highlighting positive things happening in the community caught on. Nowadays many television shows are celebrating the goodness of ordinary people.

When One Door Closes, Another Window Opens

When I experienced a detached retina, I had to stop working under the harsh television lights.

Have you noticed when God closes a door, He always opens a window? I discovered Therapeutic Touch, a hands-on process in which the practitioner senses the energy of the person through their aura. The practitioner sends healing energy to the client by working solely on the aura. I was so impressed that this type of healing served premature babies and cancer patients who couldn't be touched easily that I immediately began to take classes and subsequently became certified.

This type of healing also helped my children's bumps and bruises from their sports. They would often bring their friends home who had soccer injuries and ask me to "do my whammy" on their friend.

Then I discovered Reiki, a Japanese technique for stress reduction and relaxation that promotes healing. I decided to take it to help my eyes after my three detached retinas. When my daughter-in-law was diagnosed with cancer when she was eight months pregnant, I took the time to become a Reiki master so I could help her. Each of these healing techniques were applicable to my children's well-being, as well as my own. As a result, I completed the mind-body-spirit courses that enabled me to expand ways that I could help people more than ever!

A Course in Miracles was introduced to me through my nephew. This amazing course of study that focuses on Love versus Fear gave me an opportunity to revisit Louise Hay's admonition that forgiveness was essential to spiritual growth. A Course in Miracles gently led me to understand how the bridge from fear to love is called forgiveness. I stayed in the weekly group for over fifteen years. Do you see how the thread of helping people creates a mosaic of opportunities to learn different ways to fulfill my purpose?

Finding Purpose From Our Pain

My PhD in healing came through personal tragedy when Cyndi died in 2005. My Course in Miracles group helped me work on forgiveness of the individuals that I believed caused Cyndi's death. It was this wonderful group that encouraged me to journal. It was then that I discovered my ability to reach through the veil to my daughter and my mother for information and consolation.

With the help of a grief counselor and a wonderful editor and publisher, Lorraine Ash, my purpose became writing Celestial Conversations: Healing Relationships After Death. My childhood purpose to help my mother, grew to helping hundreds of mothers and families to find healing and closure after the death of their loved-ones. It also helped heal my broken heart.

My purpose became a full-fledged mission to help the brokenhearted, at a time when the whole world seems to be grieving. I believe that I needed to learn many ways of healing. I loved hands-on-healing, but I needed to learn to teach, to write, to speak and to offer workshops in order to help as many broken hearts as possible. The most challenging aspect of healing is helping people who are grieving. I learned at a gut level what grief was. Cyndi's death taught me the depth and breadth of grief. Caretaking anyone with a broken heart is the highest honor for a healer.

My Mission Comes Full Circle

When I returned to Glastonbury in 2017, I was given the opportunity to see that my life had different purposes at different times. The purposes created a coat of many colors. Each purpose was a different color in that coat. My visit to Glastonbury gave me laser vision of the gifts that I received as I moved forward from purpose to purpose in my life.

Now I see that my primary mission as a soul is to help heal those who were hurting on our planet. I learned different forms of healing from my childhood. My interest in healing never stopped growing, but I never saw the connection to the overall mission as I moved forward in my life.

It is my hope that I can entice you, dear reader, to look back at your own life. You need not go to Glastonbury to recognize your mission as a soul. You need only to reflect on the purposes that called you to keep moving forward. I now know that if I had a mission, everyone has a mission.

Exploring Your Spiritual Gift of Mission

If you take the time to review your life, you will discover the purposes that evolved in your own life.

Think back to your childhood and ask yourself some questions.

- Do you remember what your purposes were as a child? What drew your attention? Did you dream of becoming someone special when you grew up?
- Think back to high school and college. Follow the thread of purpose…your purpose. Does that purpose connect with the prior one? Is it an extension of your interest as a child?

Give yourself time to reflect and add to your journal. You might even find a picture album that reminds you of the people, incidents or inspirations that moved you forward into another purpose.

Take thirty days to add to this journal. Mold it like clay. Create a movie of your mind. Ask your angel for inspiration. Most of all trust your intuitive thoughts and write them down.

Discovering your mission now will give you a chance to decide if you are on track with your soul's mission. One of the common denominators I noticed in my life was that whenever I was offered a new opportunity to learn another form of healing, I took action. I took the courses. I joined the groups. I trusted my intuition. I learned how to write a book. I offered workshops. I did whatever I could to improve my healing ability. Now it's your turn.

Discover how your grief added to your mission. Discover how Gifts of Courage are woven into each purpose of your life. Discover how your compassion and faith has grown and expanded because of your grief. Reflect on how your grief intensified your soul's growth.

It is important to write down the answers. What helped your spiritual awareness expand? Can you find examples of individuals in your world who inspire you? Keep your antenna up. The examples are there.

I encourage you to pray and meditate with the intention of discovering your mission. The answers will come. It could be your neighbor. It could be Mahatma Gandhi. It could be Archbishop Fulton Sheen. It could be a relative or friend. Whoever you discover, write their names down in your journal.

Chapter 10
Suggestions for the Reader

Now that you know the 7 Spiritual Gifts, here are some other suggestions that I found helpful for healing my own broken heart and bringing me to an awareness of the gifts that God gave me as I walked my own path of grief.

Transpersonal Journaling

Journaling can be such a help with the grief process for discovering the spiritual gifts that may be hidden in your pain. Even if you have never journaled before, I encourage you to buy a journal and give it a try. I started journaling consistently in 2007. My preference is called Transpersonal Journaling.

1. **Start with a Prayer:** My routine is simple. I start with a prayer. My favorite prayer is from Unity:

   ### *"The Prayer of Protection"*
   By James Dillet Freeman

   The light of God surrounds me
   The love of God enfolds me
   The Power of God protects me
   The Presence of God watches over me
   Wherever I am, God is!

2. **Meditate:** The next part of my routine is to meditate for a short time in order to clear my monkey-mind. If you need help, I have a meditation on my website that you could use for free. www.loannemayer.com.

3. **Date the Page:** Then I date the page I am working on before I begin to write.

4. **Set Your Intention:** Next, I direct my journaling to someone beyond the veil i.e. God, my angels,

or my deceased mother and daughter. It depends on what advice I am looking for.

5. **Ask Questions:** My Transpersonal Journaling allows me to ask specific questions of specific individuals who can advise me about something that is important to me. For example, my mother helped me to understand why she was so distant and secretive with me. My daughter told me exactly what happened the night she died. Prior to that I was given no information by her husband or the police. Cyndi also gave me advice for how I could help her sons after her death. Help that made all the difference! Give it a try. Can't hurt. Might help.

The Picture Practice

1. **Find a picture:** Find a picture of yourself PRIOR to the death of your loved-one. If the picture is small, blow it up to 8 x10 inches or larger, so you can see your eyes clearly.

2. **List your earlier strengths:** Carefully look into your eyes in the picture. Reflect upon your strengths in those days. Make a list of your strengths. Be proud of yourself for noticing.

3. **Meditate on the past:** Use your insights written in the journal to meditate on your life in the past. If you are not a meditator, just take five minutes to think of how you used your strengths in those days. Write down your insights.

4. **List your past strengths:** Take each strength as a separate page or two. Write what you remember about your life in the past. How did your strength display in your life prior to your grief? (This is not a judgment process. It will

give you a baseline for discovering the Treasures in Your Grief.)

5. **Picture today:** Now take a picture of yourself today, as you travel your grief journey. Again, blow up the picture so you can really see your eyes. I am sure you can see the sorrow in those eyes. You have suffered a great deal. The eyes show your suffering.

6. **Go deeper:** Reflect upon the person that you are today. How have you changed? Write down what strengths you discover. Has your courage grown? Has your compassion expanded? Write down what you notice in your journal.

7. **Ask for feedback:** Consider asking a friend or relative to tell you how they feel you have changed since the death of your loved-one. We often don't notice the changes in our personality and demeanor.

8. Reflection:

- Reflect upon each individual growth that you have noticed and write down your insights. Take your time. Pick one insight a day. Do this over thirty days. I encourage you to consider a prayer asking for Divine Guidance before you journal and a prayer of gratitude for what you find.

- Now think about the help you received along the way. Go back to the time when your grief was raw. Who supported you through those dark days? As you remember the days that followed, who were the people who helped you through your grief?

- Write down all the names you can remember. You may find that there are more names than you expected. You can even consider the author of a book that helped you. There may be people whom you met for a short time, like the Pink Lady. Take five minutes to remember. They say we often entertain angels unaware. I say the more aware we are the more we will notice the treasures that are all around us.

9. **Join a Group:** Finally, I encourage you to join a meditation group so that you can take your discoveries into meditation as you move forward on your grief journey. I believe that when you meditate, you connect with other meditators. You join in the positive energy that meditators create. I also encourage you to include prayer. I find that when you pray, you join others energetically in prayer, which will lift you higher as you move forward on your Path of Grief.

Congratulations! You are discovering the Spiritual Gifts Hidden in Your Pain. There may be many more than seven spiritual gifts. Your soul has grown exponentially as you suffered the loss of your loved-one. Again, I suggest you journal over thirty days.

Chapter 11
Afterthoughts: Reflections of the Pink Lady

So often in my life, I had all the help I needed but I didn't know it. I was so busy looking for the help that I thought I needed that I didn't notice that what I needed was right next to me. This story is typical of many instances in my life where the help was right at my elbow. I even accepted the support, but I didn't recognize what a magical gift I was given until it was too late. I leave you with this last reflection on my visit with the Pink Lady:

It was the last day of my five days in Glastonbury, England, and I still hadn't found time to climb to the Tor. This famous landmark has come to be represented as an entrance to Avalon, the land of the fairies. The Tor is topped by St. Michael's tower, which is the best way to envision Avalon of Arthurian legend. I felt compelled to make the journey, even if I couldn't find my friend, Juliane, to join me as we planned.

I brought water and a notebook and hurried to the entrance of the Tor. The road wasn't the same as I remembered from my visit thirteen years prior. In those days, my friend, Elizabeth, and I had to move cows out of our way as we climbed the 518 feet to the top of the hill where St. Michael's Tower stands. Now I joined other tourists following a paved road, listening to their excitement about climbing the Tor.

After walking uphill for twenty minutes, I recognized that the Tor was on my right, not straight ahead of me on the top of the hill, as it had been years ago. Confused and already tired, I sat down on a rock on the side of the road to figure out what to do. "Should I give up or keep going?"

Behind me I heard a soft voice, "It does seem like a long way up to the Tor, doesn't it? But there is no rush."

I turned to the voice and saw the most stunning young woman. She was dressed in hot pink boots, hot pink jacket and skirt, and coal black hair that had been tinged with hot pink. I literally couldn't get up for a moment. "My name is Kat," shared the Pink Lady. "I have made this trip to the top over a dozen times. Would you like me to walk with you?"

I nodded my head "yes" as Kat gently lifted me up from the rock by my elbow. We walked slowly toward the entrance to the sheep's meadow that led to the base of the Tor. I didn't remember sheep.....only cows.
Kat kept talking about the view at the top of Tor. She brought back my memories of being with

Elizabeth thirteen years ago as she pointed out the incredible vision before us.

Elizabeth and I had stared at the view from St. Michaels Tower for the longest time. We felt we could almost see the lake that surrounded Avalon. We were encouraged to lay down on the grass to listen for the fairies that guarded the chalice of Christ brought by Joseph of Arimathea not long after the crucifixion of Jesus Christ. Celtic mythology claims that the fairies still guard that chalice.

Back in the present moment and catching my breath with Kat, I shared that my sixty-one-year-old legs were complaining and we hadn't even gotten to the bottom of the Tor. Over and over, Kat claimed she had all the time in the world. I was worried that I was taking too much time on my last day of visiting Glastonbury. The effort was exhausting for me. I had to stop and sit on a log or a bench quite often as we climbed upward. Each short rest was filled with Kat's stories of the last time she had come to Glastonbury or something she noticed in the far distance.

It never occurred to me that she never mentioned where she came from or where she lived. It took an hour of climbing but Kat made the trip so special that I was almost surprised when we got to the Top. We sat together on the grass for at least fifteen minutes without a word. The view was magical. We could see for miles. I felt we could see Avalon. It brought tears to my eyes.

Suddenly I heard a familiar voice: Juliane had come to the Tor by another route. There was a quicker path that had a cement path with benches that only took twenty minutes to climb. Juliane called, "There you are! So sorry I wasn't there to walk up with you." I got up to hug her for looking for me.

"Juliane, I met this wonderful new friend. You must meet her." Whispering, I said, "She is quite unique. I could never have made the climb without her." I introduced Kat to my friend. We took a picture and then I turned back to Juliane to ask how much time we had left before we had to leave Glastonbury.

When I turned back to where Kat had been standing, she was gone. The circumference of the Tower of St. Michael was only 500 ft. I ran all around the area, but I couldn't find Kat. I asked a few people if they had seen the Pink Lady. Some said "No." Some looked at me as if I were a bit crazy.

We never found Kat. The picture we took on my phone disappeared. I've come to believe that Kat was an angel who came to help me climb the Tor. She also helped me to see the beauty in the climb. She distracted me from the effort of climbing by sharing many stories that I hold in my heart to this day. Without her, I would have quit. In those days I would focus on the outcome I wanted. I didn't notice the beauty of the journey.

Kat taught me to find the beauty within the journey. I was convinced that climbing the Tor was a challenge for me without help. I wanted help. I needed help. And yet I didn't recognize that it was angelic help that walked beside me.

Just as my grief had been daunting, I needed help to move forward. Looking back, I recognize that I had lots of angelic help as I moved through my grief that I didn't recognize or accept at first:

Learning to use transpersonal journaling was just the help I needed when my mother and daughter died. Meeting a professor from a local university who told me about Transpersonal Psychology was exactly what I needed at the time. Receiving the perfect guidance counselor who didn't blink when I told her I was reaching through the veil to my loved-ones. Being guided to a wonderful Compassionate Friends group when I needed to be with people who understood grief. Having a wonderful editor and publisher for my first book, who wanted my story. People and organizations who reached out to me who wanted me to teach workshops to help the broken-hearted. Co-founding the International Grief Council with the help of friends from Israel and India. Having the opportunity to present a Grief Retreat in England that brought me back to Glastonbury thirteen years after Cyndi's death.

When I look back at The Pink Lady's visit, I realize how many times I prayed for help and it came in unexpected, even unnoticed ways. Kat changed all that for me. She helped me to understand that any journey, no matter how overwhelming it may be, can be achieved by allowing others to help, without udgment as to how the help looks. I keep that wisdom in my heart to this day.

If you look back, I guarantee that you will find that you received Treasures in Your Grief as well. Treasures that could be people, opportunities, even angels who expanded your soul as you walked your personal Path of Grief. Take the time to remember and treasure your gifts. As you move forward in your mission, your awareness will not only serve you well, but it will serve humanity as well.

Love 'n Light,

Lo Anne

About Defining Moments Press

Built for aspiring authors who are looking to share transformative ideas with others throughout the world, Defining Moments Press offers life coaches, healers, business professionals, and other non-fiction or self-help authors a comprehensive solution to getting their books published without breaking the bank or taking years.

Defining Moments Press prides itself on bringing readers and authors together to find tools and solutions.

As an alternative to self-publishing or signing with a major publishing house, we offer full profits to our authors, low-priced author copies, and simple contract terms.

Most authors get stuck trying to navigate the technical end of publishing. The comprehensive publishing services offered by Defining Moments Press mean that your book will be designed by an experienced graphic artist, available in printed, hard copy format, and coded for all eBook readers, including the Kindle, iPad, Nook, and more.

We handle all of the technical aspects of your book creation so you can spend more time focusing on your business that makes a difference for other people.

Defining Moments Press founder, publisher, and #1 bestselling author Melanie Warner has over twenty years of experience as a writer, publisher, master life coach, and accomplished entrepreneur.

You can learn more about Warner's innovative approach to self-publishing or take advantage of free trainings and education at:
MyDefiningMoments.com.

Defining Moments Book Publishing

If you're like many authors, you have wanted to write a book for a long time, maybe you have even started a book...but somehow, as hard as you have tried to make your book a priority, other things keep getting in the way.

Some authors have fears about their ability to write or whether or not anyone will value what they write or buy their book. For others, the challenge is making the time to write their book or having accountability to finish it.

It's not just finding the time and confidence to write that is an obstacle. Most authors get overwhelmed with the logistics of finding an editor, finding a support team, hiring an experienced designer, and

Lo Anne Mayer

figuring out all the technicalities of writing, publishing, marketing, and launching a book. Others have actually written a book and might have even published it but did not find a way to make it profitable.

For more information on how to participate in our next Defining Moments Author Training program, visit: www.MyDefiningMoments.com. Or you can email Melanie@MyDefiningMoments.com.

Other Books By Defining Moments Press

Defining Moments: Coping With the Loss of a Child - Melanie Warner

Defining Moments SOS: Stories of Survival - Melanie Warner and Amber Torres

Become Brilliant: Roadmap From Fear to Courage – Shiran Cohen

Unspoken: Body Language and Human Behavior For Business - Shiran Cohen

Rise, Fight, Love, Repeat: Ignite Your Morning Fire - Jeff Wickersham

Life Mapping: Decoding the Blueprint of Your Soul - Karen Loenser

Ravens and Rainbows: A Mother-Daughter Story of Grit, Courage and Love After Death – L. Grey and Vanessa Lynn

Pivot You! 6 Powerful Steps to Thriving During Uncertain Times – Suzanne R. Sibilla

A Workforce Inspired: Tools to Manage Negativity and Support a Toxic-Free Workplace – Dolores Neira

Journey of 1000 Miles: A Musher and His Huskies' Journey on the Century-Old Klondike Trails - Hank DeBruin and Tanya McCready

7 Unstoppable Starting Powers: Powerful Strategies For Unparalleled Results From Your First Year as a New Leader – Olusegun Eleboda

*Bouncing Back From Divorce With Vitality &
Purpose: A Strategy For Dads* – Nigel J Smart,
PHD

*Focus on Jesus and Not the Storm: God's Non-
negotiables to Christians in America* - Keith Kelley

*Stepping Out, Moving Forward: Songs and
Devotions* - Jacqueline O'Neil Kelley

*Time Out For Time In: How Reconnecting With
Yourself Can Help You Bond With Your Child in a
Busy Word* - Jerry Le

*The Sacred Art of Off Mat Yoga: Whisper of
Wisdom Forever* – Shakti Barnhill

*The Beauty of Change: The Fun Way For Women
to Turn Pain Into Power & Purpose* – Jean Amor
Ramoran

Lo Anne Mayer

From No Time to Free Time: 6 Steps to Work/Life Balance For Business Owners - Christoph Nauer

Self-Healing For Sexual Abuse Survivors: Tired of Just Surviving, Time to Thrive - Nickie V. Smith

Frog on a Lily Pad - Michael Lehre

How to Effectively Supercharge Your Career as a CEO - Giorgio Pasqualin

Rising From Unsustainable: Replacing Automobiles and Rockets - J.P. Sweeney

Food - Life's Gift for Healing: Simple, Delicious & Life Saving Whole Food Plant Based Solutions - Angel and Terry Grier

Harmonize All of You With All: The Leap Ahead in Self-Development - Artie Vipperla

Powerless to Powerful: How to Stop Living in Fear and Start Living Your Life - Kat Spencer

Living with Dirty Glasses: How to Clean those Dirty Glasses and Gain a Clearer Perspective Of Your Life - Leah Spelt Ligia

The Road Back to You: Finding Your Way After Losing a Child to Suicide - Trish Simonson

Gavin Gone: Turning Pain into Purpose to Create a Legacy - Rita Gladding

The Health Nexus: TMJ, Sleep Apnea, and Facial Development, Causations and Treatment - Robert Perkins DDS

Samantha Jean's Rainbow Dream: A Young Foster Girl's Adventure into the Colorful World of Fruits & Vegetables - AJ Autieri – Luciano

Live Your Truth: An Arab Man's Journey In Finding the Courage to Live His Truth As He Identifies as Gay and Coping with Mental Illness Paperback - David Rabadi

Unstoppable: A Parent's Survival Guide for Special Education Services with an IEP or 504 Plan - Raja B. Marhaba

Please, Excuse My Brave: Overcoming Fear and Living Out Your Purpose - Anisa Wesley

Drawing with Purpose : A Sketch Journal - Rick Alonzo

Good Work: How Gen X and Millennials are the Dream Team for Doing Good When Collaborating Well - Erin-Kate Whitcomb

NY Coffee: Love Fulfilled in the Little Things - Craig Lieckfelt

Made in the USA
Middletown, DE
15 November 2023

42666470R00106